ON
SOLIDARITY

Coeditor-in-Chief & Publisher Deborah Chasman

Coeditor-in-Chief Joshua Cohen

Executive Editor Matt Lord

Manuscript and Production Editor Hannah Liberman

Assistant Editor Cameron Avery

Audience Engagement Editor Ben Schacht

Associate Publisher & Fellowship Coordinator Jasmine Parmley

Marketing and Development Coordinator Irina Costache

Contributing Editors Adom Getachew, Lily Hu, Walter Johnson, Robin D. G. Kelley, Paul Pierson, Becca Rothfeld, & Simon Torracinta

Contributing Arts Editors Ed Pavlić & Ivelisse Rodriguez

Black Voices in the Public Sphere Fellows Maya Jenkins & N'Kosi Oates

Editorial Assistants Ione Barrows, Kathy Chow, & Marie Ungar

Finance Manager Anthony DeMusis III

Printer Sheridan PA

Board of Advisors Derek Schrier (Chair), Margo Beth Fleming, Archon Fung, Deborah Fung, Richard M. Locke, Jeff Mayersohn, Scott Nielsen, Robert Pollin, Rob Reich, Hiram Samel, Kim Malone Scott, Brandon M. Terry, & Michael Voss

Interior Graphic Design Zak Jensen & Alex Camlin

Cover Design Alex Camlin

Printed and bound in the United States.

Distributed by Haymarket Books (www.haymarketbooks.org) to the trade in the U.S. through Consortium Book Sales and Distribution (www.cbsd.com) and internationally through Ingram Publisher Services International (www.ingramcontent.com).

On Solidarity is *Boston Review* issue 2023.3 (Forum 27 / 48.3 under former designation system).

Kelly Hayes & Mariame Kaba's essay is adapted with permission from *Let This Radicalize You: Organizing and the Revolution of Reciprocal Care*, published in 2023 by Haymarket Books.

Image on pages 1, 8, and 9: Chicago History Museum via Getty Images

Image on page 98: Ted Polumbaum/Freedom Forum's Newseum Collection

To become a member, visit bostonreview.net/memberships.

For questions about donations and major gifts, contact Irina Costache, irina@bostonreview.net.

For questions about memberships, email members@bostonreview.net.

Boston Review
PO Box 390568
Cambridge, MA 02139

ISSN: 0734-2306 / ISBN: 978-1-946511-84-3

CONTENTS

EDITORS' NOTE
Deborah Chasman & Matt Lord

SOLIDARITY HAS long been a key idea in struggles for a more just world. What does it mean, and how can movements build enough of it to change society?

Organizer and political theorist Mie Inouye leads this issue's forum on obstacles to collective action today. "Even though we recently experienced one of the most remarkable displays of interracial solidarity in our country's history," she writes of the protests following the murder of George Floyd in 2020, "interracial solidarity—solidarity across *any* form of difference, for that matter—seems less plausible now." In the years since, debates about the role of race and class in movement spaces have suggested a cruel paradox: "On the one hand, solidarity is an essential component of struggles for justice, but on the other hand, actually existing injustice renders it impossible."

In the face of this impasse, movements have frequently turned to deference politics—a model of coalition building that asks relatively more privileged people to defer to the most marginalized. Inouye argues that this vision has made movements brittle. In place of deference, she proposes a model of organizing that embraces conflict as a form of political education and personal transformation—all in the interest of building endurance, which is key to making change. And for that, Inouye concludes, there is no substitute for the hard work of good organizing.

Eleven respondents pick up different threads of Inouye's argument. David Roediger and Sarah Schulman expand on the "antinomies" and "dilemmas" that can make solidarity so fraught. Daniel Martinez HoSang traces the cause back to neoliberalism, which splinters social relations and teaches us to express injustice in the language of personal grievance. Alex Gourevitch sees the debate as a "cipher for the problem of trust." And in different ways, Charisse Burden-Stelly, Jodi Dean, and Rev. William Barber II clarify the political stakes of social movements. In her reply, Inouye stresses how the social and political are intertwined.

Other contributors explore solidarity in specific contexts. Labor organizer Ege Yumuşak makes the case for more democracy in unions. Gaiutra Bahadur rejects the Asian exceptionalism that has obstructed multiracial solidarity. In conversation with nia t. evans, Dan Berger, Gwendolyn Zoharah Simmons, and Michael Simmons reflect on the lessons of the civil rights movement and beyond. Reviewing films about abortion, Judith Levine teases out the solidarity that emerges as reproductive rights narrow, while Simon Torracinta shows how basic income can pave the way to a more solidaristic society. Finally, veteran activists Kelly Hayes and

Mariame Kaba share what they have learned about keeping people moving toward the same goal.

Together these pieces offer a window into how social change happens. Solidarity is important, they make clear, because it is essential to movements—and movements are essential to building a more just world. As Astra Taylor and Leah Hunt-Hendrix put it, "Without solidarity, we'll remain divided, which means we're already conquered."

SOLIDARITY NOW

Mie Inouye

AT A FUNDRAISER for a political organization this spring, a first-generation Asian American organizer from a working-class background asked me, "Why do you organize?"

The organizer—call him Henry—had requested three times that I put on a name tag, and each time I had silently refused, so we were engaged in a subtle but protracted conflict. He was being friendly, but he was also trying to organize me. I answered honestly because I was irritated. "I organize because I need to organize," I said, "not really because I expect to change the world in any big ways. I just need to have meetings to go to. And I hope that through my actions I am generating possibilities that other people will take up in unexpected ways and that may actually bring about a revolution, even if not in my lifetime and not as a direct result of my actions."

"That's so interesting," he responded. "For me, it's because of the material changes my family needs to see to our lives in order to survive." I felt chastened. Only a bourgeois, fourth-generation Asian American college professor organizes for the meetings.

I immediately recognized the political power of Henry's words. Behind them lie influential left intellectual traditions that see material need as the most potent and reliable basis of solidarity. Still, something in me resisted his implicit criticism. When I consider not only my motivations for organizing but also how I learned to organize, I think of a perhaps unexpected institution: the Mormon Church. While theorists have tended to emphasize either material interest or moral commitment as the basis for solidarity, my experience growing up Mormon taught me that people organize for multiple and simultaneous reasons, sometimes opaque even to themselves. It also taught me that regularly showing up to meetings with very different people is itself a crucial basis for solidarity, at least as potent as either material need or moral commitment.

In a moment of fractious debates about the role of race and class in organizing, social endurance—the capacity to keep showing up, even when you don't like the other people in the room—might sound like a minimalist solution, too weak to meet the challenges we face. I think it harbors a radical and ambitious lesson: that you cannot know in advance what a meeting—or a struggle over a nametag—will do to you. A commitment to cultivating endurance signals your openness to being transformed, even as you work to transform others. And it helps explain, I will argue, what we most need from a theory of solidarity today.

POLITICAL THEORISTS and organizers have long debated the possible basis for solidarity in societies structured by dominance. If solidarity simply means collective action based on recognition of shared interests, it would seem that there can be no solidarity across lines of domination, as the interests of those who dominate diverge from the interests of those who are dominated.

This gap generates a cruel paradox, at least if we accept that such alliances—between dominant and dominated racial groups within the working class, say, or between the traditional working class and the so-called "professional-managerial class" (PMC)—are necessary to redress racial and economic domination in the United States. On the one hand, solidarity is an essential component of struggles for justice, but on the other hand, actually existing injustice renders it impossible. What do we do when winning material changes to the social world requires assembling coalitions of people who do not—and perhaps cannot—share the same motivations for organizing? What kind of solidarity is possible when our motivations for organizing diverge, or when we don't even know what they are?

Some theorists present morality as the way to close the gap between the interests of dominant and dominated groups. In *Race and the Politics of Solidarity* (2009), for example, political theorist Juliet Hooker argues that, in racialized societies, solidarity is also racialized. "Solidarity requires that we care about the pain and suffering of others," she writes. "But embodied racial difference renders the pain and suffering of nonwhites either invisible or, when visible, less deserving of empathy and redress." Given this reality, a prerequisite to solidarity between members of dominant and dominated racial groups is a transformation of the former's "ethical-political perspective." On this view, white people in the United States must learn to see themselves "seeing whitely." In other words, they must come to recognize that race regularly blinds them to the pain and suffering of nonwhites.

How can whites achieve this realization? For Hooker, the answer lies in public contestation over policies that could redress past and continuing disadvantage. Such contestation holds the potential to reshape the political community's public memory with regard to race. But even if public debate over policing, reparations, and abolition of the prison-industrial complex could promote the kind of moral transformation Hooker envisions, can we expect fundamental changes in behavior to follow?

In a recent article, political scientist Jared Clemons argues that it is a mistake to think that even the most sincerely felt antiracism will translate into antiracist behavior under neoliberal capitalism. Clemons's premise is that the recognition of shared class interests with Black Americans is a precondition of whites' long-term commitment to substantive antiracist policies. Morality is not irrelevant, Clemons thinks, but moral commitment alone is insufficient. Unfortunately, he argues, neoliberal capitalism has undermined the conditions for such recognition in two crucial ways.

First, it has "privatized racial responsibility," predisposing white people—particularly white liberal members of the PMC—to make merely symbolic antiracist commitments that do not threaten their dominant class position or social status, rather than supporting state programs that would address structural racial injustices. At the same time, Clemons argues that the white PMC is currently much more readily available to movements for racial justice than the white working class. He cites Martin Luther King, Jr.'s Poor People's Campaign and *A "Freedom Budget" for All Americans* (1967), written by A. Phillip Randolph and Bayard Rustin, as examples of the kind of multiracial, working-class coalitions necessary to achieve a material transformation of society, but he is pessimistic about the possibility that such coalitions will emerge under present conditions. The gap between the interests of participants in recent movements for racial justice is just too wide.

Clemons's careful attention to the material conditions of neoliberal capitalism and their implications for solidarity is useful. But if he is right that the white PMC is the most accessible base of white Americans for today's movements for racial and economic justice, then a thoroughgoing materialist analysis should identify not only avenues for organizing the traditional white working class, but also ways of working with the contradictions of the PMC.

What seems crucial to this effort is not that everyone involved in today's movements share the same motivations or even the same objective interests but that everyone have something at stake that they feel viscerally. In an interview with Stevphen Shukaitis, Fred Moten highlights the role of personal stakes in the concept of coalition embraced by the original Rainbow Coalition—the cross-racial movement forged by Fred Hampton (of the Black Panthers), William Fesperman (of the socialist, mostly white Young Patriots Organization), and

José Cha Cha Jiménez (of the predominantly Puerto Rican Young Lords). As Moten puts it:

> The problematic of coalition is that coalition isn't something that emerges so that you can come help me, a maneuver that always gets traced back to your own interests. The coalition emerges out of your recognition that it's fucked up for you, in the same way that we've already recognized that it's fucked up for us. I don't need your help. I just need you to recognize that this shit is killing you, too, however much more softly, you stupid motherfucker, you know?

For the reasons Clemons gives, we might doubt the possibility of interest convergence ("it's fucked up for you, in the same way that . . . it's fucked up for us"), depending on the class position of the imagined white interlocutor. But note that Moten's emphasis is on shared "recognition," not shared conditions of domination or oppression. In other words, the sameness he describes applies to the process of realization, not to the interests of the people involved. The promise of coalition is that we can work together across difference to change the prevailing social arrangement without fully transcending the ways that it differentiates us and even pits us against each other.

Maybe a better basis for solidarity than either morality or material interest, then—at least around racial injustice in the United States today—is ideology: a shared vision of a just society that aligns with but exceeds our material interests, that motivates us both because it would make our lives tangibly better and because we find it inspiring and attractive. This seems to be what political theorist Jodi Dean has in mind when she writes in *Comrade: An*

Essay on Political Belonging (2019) that "comradeship binds action, and in this binding . . . it collectivizes and directs action in light of a shared vision for the future." This kind of shared vision does not materialize out of our individual pursuits, nor does it emerge from protest alone. And, as Moten's open expression of antipathy toward his imagined comrade suggests, forging such a vision across difference necessarily involves conflict.

IN JUNE 2020, I, like millions of other Americans, left the isolation of my apartment, where I had been watching footage of the Minneapolis protests, to join other breathing, sweating bodies in the streets. We were in the streets to protest the murders of George Floyd, Breonna Taylor, and Ahmaud Arbery, among many other Black Americans. But we were also there because we were dying of being alone and we needed to be pressed up against each other in a crowd. We were there because we were unemployed or facing the prospect of unemployment, because our jobs were killing us, because we or our loved ones were sick and dying and the state was indifferent to our plight. And we were there because we felt that these reasons were somehow connected to each other and to Floyd's death. But forging those connections explicitly would have involved conflict, risk, and time. It was easier and safer to default to "allyship" or even a straight-up politics of deference.

I often ask my students what the summer of 2020 was like for them. For almost all of them, it was their first and only experience of a social movement. Some describe being in a crowd of people who were blocking a highway or a bridge and realizing, for the first time in their lives, that everyone around them was sincere in what they were doing. Others describe experiences of tear gas and tanks that gave them a visceral understanding of the state's repressive power.

But another feeling my students express in the wake of 2020 is a deep skepticism about the possibility or even desirability of solidarity across difference. Even though we recently experienced one of the most remarkable displays of interracial solidarity in our country's history, interracial solidarity—and solidarity across any form of difference, for that matter—seems less plausible now than it did before 2020. There are many enduring legacies of the George Floyd rebellions, but I think we can say that a sustained multiracial movement against policing and mass incarceration is not among them.

Could it have been otherwise? It is a common folly of left intellectuals and organizers to critique movements for not having been differently composed or executed. As Frances Fox Piven and Richard Cloward famously argue in *Poor People's Movements* (1977), opportunities for protest are socially structured. Popular insurgency "flows from historically specific circumstances," they write: "it is a reaction against those circumstances, and it is also limited by those circumstances." It is therefore futile to critique movements for failing to conform to our theories about how protest ought to proceed. Still, the point of organizing, as I understand it, is to prepare to make the most of socially structured opportunities for protest. And in preparation for the next opportunity, the left needs to build more organizations in which differently situated people can uncover and articulate their needs and forge demands that connect them. We also need to find an approach to the problem of divergent interests that accepts the insights of standpoint theory without defaulting to deference.

The best text I have found on the process of uncovering needs through organizing is the footage of Illinois Black Panther Party section leader Bob Lee organizing white working-class people in Chicago in the 1969 documentary *American Revolution 2*. As Jakobi Williams details in *From the Bullet to the Ballot* (2015), the Illinois Black Panthers used this documentary, produced by The Film Group, to found the Rainbow Coalition and to teach their organizing model to other chapters.

The most compelling part of the documentary is a scene where Lee comes to a meeting in the Uptown neighborhood of Chicago organized by the Young Patriots. The purpose of the gathering is to organize the Patriots' base to disrupt an upcoming meeting about the Model Cities program, a federal antipoverty initiative that the Patriots felt shut out community input. Lee works the room with incredible skill. Repeatedly, he asks the white people, who look awkward and even a little scared, "What do you want?"

When I ask my students to identify the tactics Lee uses to organize the people in the room, they note his use of physical proximity and touch. Lee is always on his feet, moving around the room and touching his interlocutors. At one point, he places his hands in the hair of a sixteen-year-old white boy named Roger who declares his desire to fight the police. In this moment, Lee's hands express care and authority, reminding the boy of his youth and inexperience. "Before you can do that," he says, "there's got to be some discipline." At another moment, Lee's hands are on the shoulders of a middle-aged white man who sits with his arms crossed and looks uncomfortable. Later, they grasp the hands of a reticent young white woman with a toddler. Lee eventually lifts the woman to her feet and insists that she tell the room what she's been going through. She finally speaks, and, as she describes witnessing her brother being stabbed in the back by a cop, her facial expression changes from fear to confidence and conviction.

I think my students are struck by the physicality of Lee's approach to organizing because touching strangers in this way is completely unimaginable to them. In the same way, it is hard for them to imagine disagreeing openly with strangers or insisting that other people share their experiences of oppression. But what is solidarity if not the choice to bump up against other people, figuratively, if not literally, and allow oneself to be changed by the impact?

When I asked my students why they thought Lee insisted that the young white woman speak, a non-white student from a working-class background responded, "Because she needed to figure out why she was there." I left class wondering what it would take for my students to be able to ask each other, "Why are you taking this class on *Identity Politics*? What do you want?" and for all of them, including those who were white and upper-middle-class, to know and share their answers.

LEE'S APPROACH to multiracial organizing stands in stark contrast to deference politics, an approach to coalition building that requires relatively privileged people to accept less privileged people's reasons for organizing as their own. Perhaps for the sorts of reasons Clemons identifies, deference politics has become the dominant approach to coalition building in our moment.

Deference politics is also the dominant practical application of standpoint theory, which originates in Marxist feminist and Black feminist thought. The basic premises of standpoint theory are as follows. First, knowledge is socially situated; it reflects the perspective of the knower, which, in turn, is shaped by their social location. Second, oppressed groups are socially located in ways that can make it easier for them to understand how society is structured, to expose existing social arrangements as contingent, and to analyze those arrangements in relation to universal human interests. And third, dominant groups are socially situated in ways that can make it easier for them to analyze the social world in relation to dominant group interests and to misrepresent existing social arrangements as necessary, natural, or universally beneficial.

As philosopher Olúfẹ́mi Táíwò argues in *Elite Capture* (2022), these premises are difficult to dispute. Experiences of oppression tend to predispose people to develop critiques of existing social arrangements and insights into possible alternatives. At the same time, Táíwò observes, oppression does not necessarily yield strategic insight, political wisdom, or clarity about one's own motives and interests; the harm it produces can also be incapacitating. Moreover, people are capable of developing knowledge that transcends their own lived experience through studying, organizing, and getting to know differently situated people, and no person is fully knowable on the basis of even the most fine-grained analysis of their social location.

From this perspective, the problem with deference politics is not its appeal to the premises of standpoint theory but its application of them: the tendency to treat people as fully determined, rather than only influenced, by their social location—and to assume we are fully transparent to ourselves and to others.

Still, deference politics can be attractive, in part because it can serve as a tool for evading conflict. If my perspective is irrelevant, there is no chance that you and I will have salient disagreements over our shared goals or the best means of achieving them. If I am relatively privileged, acknowledging and discrediting my perspective in advance insulates me from being accused of racism, sexism, or classism—as well as from the awkwardness of disagreeing with someone who is relatively oppressed. But coalitions formed through deference are also extremely fragile, because, as Moten suggests, the perspective of the relatively privileged person is not irrelevant. It will inevitably emerge in the process of organizing. If an organization lacks the capacity to negotiate conflicts between divergent perspectives, it will quickly dissolve. Moreover, unless people know why they are at the protest or meeting and feel the stakes of their participation viscerally, they won't stick around through the inevitable setbacks and frustrations involved in organizing.

The past few years have given us some very useful critiques of deference politics, Táíwò's among them. What's lacking, I think, is a practical alternative to that takes seriously the essential insight of standpoint theory—that social location influences what we can know about the social world, and, in particular, about the sources of and potential means of countering oppression. Táíwò offers "constructive politics"—collective attempts to build "power in and through institutions and networks"—as an alternative to deference politics. Where deference politics focuses our energies on redistributing power within "the room" in which we find ourselves (a boardroom, a university, a neighborhood association, a union, and so on), constructive politics aims to "build a new house." But constructive politics does not necessarily involve attending to the ways social location influences knowledge. Think, for example, of approaches to labor organizing that are inattentive to the roles of race, gender, or sexuality in the organization of the workplace. Knowledge about intersecting forms of oppression is crucial to getting the right answers about what kinds of houses we ought to build—and to acknowledging and responsibly navigating the power dynamics within the room in the meantime.

Perhaps epistemic humility is an alternative practical application of standpoint theory. To be epistemically humble is to hold one's beliefs about the social world open to challenge and reformulation, while retaining the ultimate responsibility for judgment. Epistemic humility requires that we acknowledge that our perspectives are limited, that we cannot fully see their contours in advance, and that we are capable of understanding beyond the limits of our own lived experience. If we are open to the possibility that we might be wrong about important things and, in many ways, ill-equipped to be good comrades because of our own past experiences, we can learn from one another's experiences and from the experience of organizing together. In other words, solidarity becomes possible when we embrace organizing as a mechanism of political education, a way of being transformed, for everyone involved—dominated and dominator; Black, Asian, and white; working-class and PMC.

HENRY'S QUESTION at the spring fundraiser helped me clarify my own reasons for organizing, which begin with my family. My Japanese family became American by way of Mormonism, which was the form of solidarity available to them in the aftermath of World War II, when my great-grandparents and their children were interned in Wyoming. Through the internment, they lost their farms, their homes, and a generation of accumulated wealth.

My grandparents met, married, and had their first child in the camp. After they were released, they relocated to a small agricultural community in central Utah. Like many Nisei who had been interned, they did their best to assimilate; they named their children after American presidents and didn't teach them Japanese. They rarely spoke about the camp except to recall their wedding banquet. And although they were practicing Buddhists, they sent their children to the Mormon church so that they would get religious training and learn how to be Americans.

The church helped my family to survive the brutality of racial capitalism, primarily by providing us with a sense of belonging and a network that helped my father and his siblings succeed socially, academically, and professionally. My father often recalls the first church social he ever attended. Each guest received a giant sugar cookie frosted with a thick layer of pink buttercream. This cookie—a staple of Mormon food culture—seemed to my five-year-old father as big as his head. It tasted like nothing his Sansei tongue had ever encountered. The fact that he, a small Japanese boy whose family had recently arrived in Utah, had been given one of his own meant that he, too, belonged.

At the same time that it gave us a community, the church facilitated my family's assimilation to what Daniel Martinez HoSang, in his recent book *A Wider Type of Freedom* (2021), calls "Caucasian democracy"—"an approach to governance that takes human hierarchy, the accumulation of profit, and the unequal distribution of life and death as core premises." Mormons were not always on board with this form of democracy. In the nineteenth century they practiced a version of socialism called the United Order, and some prominent leaders were abolitionists (although the church was in many respects racist and, from 1852 to 1978, official church policy was anti-Black). But by the time that my family joined the church, Mormons were well into the process of assimilating into mainstream American society, including American capitalism. The church offered my family an ideology that linked private wealth accumulation and the heteronormative family to U.S. citizenship, and gave them hope in their ability to achieve not only eternal life but the American Dream.

My childhood in the Northeast was far removed from these sites of trauma and assimilation, but I felt this history when I visited Utah each summer—in my family's intense work ethic, in my uncles' reactionary political views, which eventually led some of them to embrace Trumpism, and in my uncles' and aunties' misdirected bursts of anger.

My uncle (I will call him Gerald here), the patriarch of our family, exemplified all of these tendencies—and a certain version of solidarity, too. Gerald was the only family member of my father's generation to stay in the small rural town where they grew up. He did not return to the farm, as my grandfather had hoped someone would; instead he became a rural doctor and dedicated himself to providing affordable health care to the community, often footing the bill for patients who could not afford to pay. He raised the funds to build a new middle school in town and mentored many generations of local youth.

Uncle Gerald's generosity was matched by his intolerance of deviations from the social norms that structured our family. When, as children, we scraped our knees while working on the farm or recreating in the mountains, we knew never to cry or complain for fear of being mocked. When, as an adult, I wrote an op-ed in the *Salt Lake Tribune* urging Mormons to stop paying tithing to the church until its leadership reversed a homophobic policy, I learned through a cousin that Uncle Gerald was furious that I would presume to tell him what to do.

In December 2020 Uncle Gerald died of COVID-19. On one level, his death, like every coronavirus death, was an avoidable consequence of the capitalist system that produced the pandemic and the state's failure to manage it. At the same time, his personality and ideological orientation, including his recklessness, his libertarian leanings, and his fierce loyalty to his community, made him particularly vulnerable to the virus and to premature death. When his friend, the local dentist, got COVID-19 and requested a home visit, Uncle Gerald went—maskless—without a second thought. When he contracted the virus and developed symptoms, he chose to treat himself at home rather than go to the hospital, and the first treatment he tried was hydroxychloroquine. By the time he finally allowed my aunt to drive him to the hospital, he could barely breathe.

I often wonder what might have happened to my family if we had encountered a different form of solidarity in the wake of internment, one that was not so closely tethered to the American Dream. Would Uncle Gerald have lived a longer life? Could he have been a participant in the Black Lives Matter movement, rather than a skeptical onlooker, afraid of identifying too closely with what he called "victim mentality"? What kind of an organization might allow my family to identify racial capitalism as the root cause of our internment and my uncle's premature death, and to find common cause with others who have an interest in transforming that system? Perhaps another answer to Henry's question is that I organize because the same shit that killed George Floyd killed my Uncle Gerald, however more softly and however more self-inflicted, and because I, too, want my family to survive.

THE VISION OF togetherness animating Mormonism is one of permanent unity—the formation of an "eternal family," whose persistence depends on rigid hierarchies, the suppression of internal conflict, and the exclusion of those who might threaten the group's stability. In this respect, Mormonism resembles what political theorist Nathan DuFord, in their recent book *Solidarity in Conflict* (2022), calls "antisocial solidarity": forms of solidarity that ultimately undermine the necessary conditions for common life by cultivating domination and exclusion.

What does it look like to organize without aspiring to unity or permanence? DuFord argues that solidarity, when it is democratic, is always premised on disunity, because conflict within solidarity organizations serves as a crucial check on domination and exclusion. On this point, DuFord articulates a version of the paradox of divergent interests: "Often, solidarity organizations reproduce the exclusions and injustices from the situation in which they are formed. This is not a condemnation, but simply evidence that these organizations do not exist outside the material context in which they are formed." Given this reality, the only way to make such organizations less exclusive is for members to agitate for change from within.

While we tend to associate neoliberalism with individualism and, therefore, with selfishness and conflict over scarce resources, DuFord shows that neoliberalism actually tends to produce a certain sort of consensus. Good neoliberal subjects assume agreement about existing economic and political arrangements and leave each other alone, rather than confronting each other and trying to change each other's minds. In this way, neoliberal society tends to drive us apart. By contrast, DuFord suggests that conflict within solidarity organizations transforms the neoliberal subject into "a member of a society." For DuFord, internal conflict takes "what was initially an individual goal a person perhaps thought many others shared, and transforms the goal, the person, and that person's norms." Through conflict, our understandings of our own interests and the world we want to build can change. At the same time, we can become more knowledgeable, less dominating, less judgmental, and more generous in our interpretations of one another—in a word, more cooperative.

Of course, even if conflict can be productively transformative, it doesn't always have that effect. Many conflicts simply make people never want to go to another meeting again. If one product of neoliberalism is consensus, another seems to be a particular style of conflict: one that atomizes, rather than transforms, the people involved.

Recognizing this fact, DuFord attempts to distinguish between constructive and destructive conflict. Following sociologists Lewis Coser and George Simmel, DuFord identifies the former sort of conflict with "realistic" disagreements, in the sense that "something real is at stake"—strategic or "substantive" issues that are "generated in the course of advancing a constitutive aim." As an example, we might think of ongoing conflicts within the Democratic Socialists of America over how socialists ought to engage in electoral politics. By contrast, "unrealistic conflict" is "generated for the purely psychological satisfaction of a fight"—it arises from "incompatible personalities or petty quarrels" and "lacks any true goal." This distinction may be plausible in principle, but it is less plausible in practice. Often what seem like strategic disagreements are also personality-based conflicts. Moreover, the latter can be constructive if we accept that our personalities are shaped by our experiences of the social world and allow even these types of disputes to work on us.

A more promising way to facilitate solidarity through conflict might be to think about the norms and practices that cultivate endurance. No conflict is productive without a social context that holds people together long enough that they have to try to understand where the other person is coming from. If we don't have to stay in the room together, we have no reason to do the difficult work of identifying the roots of our disagreement, considering the ways our experiences of privilege or oppression might be shaping our perspective, and exercising our judgment to resolve the dispute. The crucial question, then, is not how to categorize conflict as good or bad, but how to cultivate the capacity to show up when you don't know what kind of a fight it's going to be.

What's missing from DuFord's account, in other words, is the temporal dimension of solidarity. DuFord sometimes seems to suggest that stability is irrelevant to the question of how constructive conflict can be. They write, "These [internal] conflicts do threaten the groups' stability, but solidarity organizations are not intended to be permanent political institutions." Solidarity organizations are not meant to exist forever, and the attempt to make them do so produces perverse results. "Solidarity Forever" is a dangerous promise and a recipe for exclusion and domination. But solidarity organizations do have to endure for a while. The challenge is to figure out how to stick together long enough for conflict to effect change in the people involved, and in the world.

In this regard, Mormons have something that most neoliberal subjects lack—social endurance, or the capacity to keep showing up even when doing so is unpleasant. Growing up Mormon in the Boston area, I learned how to show up to three hours of meetings on Sundays, two hours of youth group on Wednesday night, and an hour of scripture study before school every morning that I didn't sleep through my alarm, all with people who I mostly did not like. Over time I came to value the frustration I experienced in these meetings. Church was the one place in my life where I regularly interacted with people who were very different from me. My friends at school were all upper-middle class, Ivy League–bound, secular, and liberal. My brothers and sisters at church were from diverse socioeconomic backgrounds. Some were recent immigrants. Many were ideologically right-wing. Most believed things that I found deeply implausible. The process of learning to work with these people to do mutual aid and organize our congregation forced me out of myself in ways that I found difficult to leave.

It should be easier to leave a democratic solidarity organization than it was for me to leave Mormonism. But some degree of social endurance is essential to both personal and social transformation, given how difficult it is to hold subjects of neoliberalism together for any length of time.

TO CULTIVATE social endurance is to enter every collective in anticipation of annoyance and heartbreak. We are going to irritate and disappoint each other, despite our best intentions. Given the ways our society is segregated by race, class, and other demographic categories, we almost certainly will find things to dislike when we get together, even if only because we don't know how to act around each other. We might even think our comrades are stupid motherfuckers, which—let's be honest—they often are. Fortunately, as Dean argues, one of the distinctive features of comradeship is that we don't have to like the people with whom we are in solidarity. Maybe political relationships work best when we don't like each other, and when we express our frustrations, disagreements, and anger with the intent of moving toward a shared goal.

To cultivate social endurance is also to value conflict as a potential site of transformation. This doesn't mean that we should actively seek conflict. But it does mean that we should not avoid necessary conflict. And when conflict arises and we find ourselves feeling chastened or annoyed, perhaps we can learn to interpret our discomfort as a process of becoming less racist, less classist, less transphobic, less judgmental, more flexible, more knowledgeable, and, ultimately, more useful to the project of building the world we want to share.

POLITICS IS MISSING

Jodi Dean

MY FIRST BOOK, *Solidarity of Strangers: Feminism After Identity Politics*, came out in 1996. The unfortunate subtitle—identity politics is still with us, for better or worse—is only one of the many things I'd change if I were writing the book today. I wouldn't change the argument that identity doesn't determine politics. As is now widely recognized, people sharing ascribed identities have profound political disagreements. Nor would I change the definition of reflective solidarity that I developed as an alternative to conventional and affective solidarities: "the mutual expectation of a responsible orientation toward relationship." Reflective solidarity still seems like a morally defensible approach to social ties, especially when differentiated in terms of the contexts within which one appeals to others for solidarity, as I explore in the book.

What I would change is the abstraction that lets me make general claims about law, democracy, inclusion, recognition and the like. In a work that aimed to contribute to political theory, politics is missing. Solidarity appears as a social rather than a political value linked to struggles for power.

Mie Inouye also treats solidarity as a social value. She admires the "social endurance" cultivated by the Mormon church even as she criticizes its hierarchical vision of unity and permanence. Her emphases on epistemic humility, understanding where people are coming from, and the value of conflict treat solidarity as a matter of interpersonal relationships, dependent on individual attitudes and the willingness to tolerate a little discomfort. With examples from religion and diversity, equity, and inclusion (DEI) best practices (my term, not Inouye's), solidarity appears as the social texture of community.

Politics emerges from gaps and frays in this texture. The gaps expose fundamental divisions: the social world is not a solidary whole. It consists of entrenched patterns of coercion, exploitation, and violence. Some of us feel compelled to join a side in the struggle over these divisions. Discipline, courage, and unity are necessary if we are to win. Those who are fighting for the other side, for a fundamentally opposed vision of the world, are excluded from our side. That's what being on the other side means.

What, then, if we emphasize not social but political endurance as a critical component of left politics? Inouye's posing of the question of commitment in a society fragmented by forty years of neoliberal capitalism pinpoints a key challenge we face on the left: how to organize for enduring political struggle on a rapidly overheating planet wrought by imperialism and oppression.

The basic menu of forms of political organization includes electoral parties and coalitions, movements, issue-based campaigns, NGOs, agitational groups, and revolutionary organizations. These different forms have varying levels of capacity and viability, generally dependent on the ability to command resources (whether these resources involve money, people, or attention). Obviously, not every political organization aims to overthrow the existing political economic system. Most seek to make changes within the existing system.

Enduring over the long haul is particularly challenging for movements and radical political associations. Movements ebb and flow; the spontaneity that generates enthusiasm resists channeling into routines and institutions. Radical politics demands enormous commitment; even the most dedicated organizers burn out. Revolutionaries face repression from the state, police harassment, and legal persecution.

To these challenges we should add the unique problems that arise from social media: argument without accountability, the seduction of the viral hot take, and the brutal pleasures that accrue from demonstrating others' weaknesses. The reflexes honed online are ill-suited to the patient, focused, and mundane work of politics—making placards, doing follow-up calls, arranging events, finding a meeting time and location, distributing fliers, and so on. People who are intellectually or affectively attracted by revolutionary ideals may lack the disposition for sustained organizational labor.

When left politics looks like movement without results, whether as fiercely ineffectual online debates or as inspiring mass demonstrations that end with the election and reelection of the same old incumbents, it's hard to feel that showing up makes a difference. In some of the 2020 protests I joined, after hours of marches, chants, and standoffs with the police, organizers would thank the crowd for coming out and remind us to vote. If voting was the answer, why did we spend the past seven hours pressed against barricades in front of the police station?

Real material factors such as working two jobs, caring for friends and family, trying to get through school, wariness of encountering the police, and basic transportation make a difference in a large country with sprawling cities and decaying infrastructure. Time is precious. Part of the challenge of political endurance is providing people with the sense that organizing is worth their time. People show up when they think showing up matters.

In her indispensable *The Romance of American Communism* (1977), Vivian Gornick recounts a story that a woman named Belle told about her seventy-year-old father. One snowy night, although bone tired, he got ready to go back out into the cold to attend a rally at Madison Square Garden. Belle tried to convince him to stay home. Her father's response: "If I don't go, who will be there?" A committed member of the Communist Party, he believed in showing up. He didn't think, "Oh well, there will be so many people there, one more won't make a difference," or "It's just another rally, so what." His party, his comrades, expected him to show up, and he expected this of himself.

Political endurance is strengthened by purpose and practice. Strong political organizations give people a reason to show up. They explain what they are fighting against and what they are fighting for. They clarify why the fight matters. The Communist Party in its heyday was enormously skilled at drawing the connections between specific issues and the long-term fight for socialism. Claudia Jones's famous International Women's Day speech from 1950 is a great example. She linked present struggles of progressive and Communist women with the traditions of the great antislavery fighters Harriet Tubman and Sojourner Truth, the militant textile workers of 1848, and women's rights pioneers Susan B. Anthony and Elizabeth Cady Stanton. Jones didn't worry about the differences between them. She drew a centuries-long arc of courage and commitment. The immediate political goal was unity. The fight was for peace, equality, and liberation which depended on organizing Black and white women in the struggle for socialism. Jones embraced her listeners with world-historical purpose. Everyone counts in the battle against the H-bomb, fascism, and imperialism.

The challenge of political endurance on the left today is that people don't know what they are fighting for. In recent decades, millions of people in the United States have come out to protest what they're against—the World Trade Organization, the Iraq War, Wall Street, racist police murder. The movements weaken as they fail to give shape to a vision of what they're for—what does winning look like? The advantage of organizations like the old Communist Party is that they articulated such a vision: every local struggle and specific issue gets its energy and purpose from the broader communist horizon.

Correct practice is essential to political endurance. These days the jargon in left organizing spaces is indistinguishable from corporate human resource departments. Disagreements are treated as identity differences. Preoccupation with interpersonal conflicts and individual discomfort displaces attention away from political work. Political organizations that orient their practices around their goals—that make clear that people have joined a political struggle that requires discipline and unity (not a social club)—navigate interpersonal issues by linking action to purpose. The old Communist parties called this practice democratic centralism. Comrades debate, vote, and accept the decision of the majority. Because keeping everyone together is so important, debate is conducted with an eye to generating unity—not scoring points, blowing off steam, or demonstrating one's knowledge of theoretical arcana.

Times have changed. We live in the shadow of the defeat of twentieth-century communism. Perhaps that's why churches and DEI best practices, ethics and economics, have eclipsed the party in our political imaginary—they reflect the world we're in. To avoid repeating the assumptions of defeat, we should learn from the purpose and practice of another time, a time when people recognized that political struggle required dedication and commitment. This can inspire us to build again the political form whose absence shapes our present: the revolutionary party. If we believe our own analyses of exploitation, oppression, and inequality, anything less is giving up.

CONTINGENT COALITIONS
Juliet Hooker

TWO IMPORTANT, longstanding questions lie behind Mie Inouye's reflections on solidarity. One is about the sources of solidarity: what motivates people to act collectively on behalf of shared political projects. The other is about the practice of solidarity: how to build it across difference, particularly for members of dominant groups.

On the first question, Inouye argues that the two dominant accounts of motivation—material interests and morality—are insufficient. A more promising basis, she proposes, is ideology: a shared vision of a just society that aligns with but exceeds narrow material interests. Such shared visions could inspire broad, enduring coalitions of differently situated people with divergent interests, she suggests, but they will not emerge solely from participation in protests, and they necessarily involve conflict. Organizing spaces where participants can disagree with each other yet work together are vital.

I agree with Inouye that genuine political solidarity is always solidarity across difference, but it is not clear how this understanding of ideology solves the problem of motivation to act in concert. Drawing on Iris Marion Young's concept of "differentiated solidarity," I've argued that rather than requiring mutual identification—that we think of others as being "like us"—solidarity is more usefully thought of as "the product of structural conditions that require people to develop contingent solidarities, however momentarily, every day." Structural conditions constrain how we relate to each other, as do the moral or ethical orientations we develop in response to them—how we diagnose the problems with our world and what we come to see as the solutions to them. This account of solidarity is consistent with the idea that it does not require unity nor sameness, at least not permanently.

Consider an example. As devastating climate disasters unfold across the globe, there are still many who deny the reality of climate change and are determined to resist or roll back green energy policies. In these conditions, some are moved to action; others accept the role of climate change but don't alter their individual behavior, join a movement, or demand more from their elected officials; still others actively resist climate justice initiatives and support politicians wedded to fossil fuels. Even among those who agree that we need to take measures to preserve the planet, there can be profound disagreements about how to do so. Some conservationists object to mega renewable energy projects such as wind farms on the grounds that they do not want local landscapes destroyed. Some environmental activists oppose the installation of electric vehicle charging stations because they think we should be moving away from car culture. In these cases, the obstacle to concerted political action is not lack of a shared vision—all want a greener, more sustainable future, without fossil fuels—but disagreements about how best to achieve it. Whether these actors work together will depend on contingent circumstances and the choices they make about how to reconcile conflicting priorities.

Inouye is well aware of these challenges, which is why she argues we need to build spaces that embrace conflict and disagreement. This brings us to the second question: how to exercise solidarity in practice. On this front, Inouye rejects the "deference politics" so prevalent in coalition-building efforts today. Coalitions based on deference are fragile, she argues, because people who see themselves as acting on behalf of others, rather than having skin in the game, quickly become disillusioned with organizing. Indeed, Inouye argues that despite the remarkable displays of interracial solidarity during the 2020 racial justice protests, her students express "deep skepticism about the possibility or even desirability of solidarity across difference." Nevertheless, such alliances are still being formed. In the Stop Cop City protests in Atlanta, for example, a broad coalition of environmental groups, neighborhood associations, local colleges, and racial justice organizations have come together to oppose the construction of a new police training center and the resulting decimation of the South River (or Weelaunee) Forest, both of which would disproportionately affect Black residents.

In the case of collective political action for racial justice in the United States today, I think the problem is not simply the one that Jared Clemons identifies—that neoliberal capitalism precludes meaningful antiracist action by white liberal professionals (who tend to support only symbolic measures) and the white working class (among whom union membership, which moderates racial prejudice, has declined significantly)—but also that moments of seeming racial progress in the United States have always been met with fierce racist backlash. The civil rights victories of the past faced immediate efforts to hollow them out. In 1967, as he contemplated the aftermath of Black rebellions in Northern cities and the hostile reception to his own efforts to organize for racial justice in Chicago, the Rev. Martin Luther King, Jr. noted that symbolic antiracism was far easier to accept than material transformation. "The great majority of Americans," he argued,

> are uneasy with injustice but unwilling yet to pay a significant price to eradicate it. . . . The persistence of racism in depth and the dawning awareness that Negro demands will necessitate structural changes in society have generated a new phase of white resistance in North and South. . . . demands that yesterday evoked admiration and support, today—to many—have become tiresome, unwarranted and a disturbance to the enjoyment of life.

Such resistance is resurgent today. White grievance has arisen (and been mobilized for reactionary political ends) in response to both symbolic antiracism—such as the casting of nonwhite actors to play characters in popular film and TV franchises—and measures that have greater material impact, such as affirmative action. White Americans from a range of economic backgrounds experience both sorts of measures as a loss. If the racial justice protests of 2020 did not produce an enduring national multiracial movement against policing and mass incarceration, it is partly because of the sustained racist backlash they *did* elicit.

At the same time, the protests should not be considered a failure, given their powerful role in transforming political imaginations and shaping ethical orientations. Political scientist Deva Woodly has argued that this is one of the key ways that social movements revitalize democracy and bring about social change. In *Reckoning* (2021), she argues that the Movement for Black Lives centers a politics of care that will require "new social, economic, and political formations . . . [that] should serve to enable not only or primarily equality, but, most importantly, must facilitate the ability to live and thrive." Part of what the 2020 protests did was disseminate a vision of a state that does not simply punish, imprison, and kill but rather creates the conditions for Black people to thrive; we see a similar claim about what is required for people to thrive in the current upsurge in labor organizing in the United States. Amid the structural conditions of profound racial injustice, this is a powerful means through which solidarity is forged.

MORAL FUSION
William J. Barber II

WHEN I RAN for president of the North Carolina NAACP in 2006, my campaign slogan was "From Banquets to Battle." We were the oldest antiracist organization in the country, I told our branches, but often we contradicted our own founding and limited ourselves as a Black organization.

Furthermore, we'd settled into traditions of celebrating the past and didn't have a clear vision of what was at stake in the present. The United States was quickly becoming a nation where white people were going to be one among many minorities, but old fears and vested interests were allied in pitting us against one another to undermine the promises of democracy. If we could come together and learn to fight together across lines drawn to divide us, we had the potential to shift the moral narrative, birth a movement, build a new voting coalition that could elect a governing majority committed to the common good, and seed that vision to the South and the whole nation. But we had to be clear: we were up against forces that did not want this solidarity, and they were willing to subvert democracy and dismantle public institutions to protect their power.

I won the election and went to work, but we didn't go out singing "Solidarity Forever" and expect a coalition to join. Instead, we asked, "Solidarity for what?" I made the case that we needed to build a broad fusion coalition, one modeled on North Carolina's and the Southern Fusion movement after Reconstruction and the broad fusion coalitions that formed during the civil rights movement. It was a struggle to get people on board, even within the NAACP. But I went to visit with the leaders of groups committed to education, health care access, workers' rights, voting rights, LGBTQ rights, women's rights, and environmental justice. I asked them all the same question: Who's preventing you from getting what you want? I watched them nod their heads as I told them that other groups had named the same adversaries.

Within a year, we built the Forward Together Moral Movement coalition and marched with thousands of people to the statehouse. Our new solidarity allowed us to successfully lobby the state legislature to raise the minimum wage and expand access to the ballot by providing a two-week period of early voting with same-day registration. In 2008 these voting laws played a key role in electing Barack Obama, who lost on Election Day itself but won thanks to early voting, along with a progressive governor and attorney general. But our real victory wasn't electing any particular candidate; it was revealing that we had built a new coalition that had the power to change the political calculus for the whole country.

Looking back, I find it striking that our adversaries paid more attention to this victory than our potential allies did. Progressive organizing groups and the Democratic Party didn't immediately invest in coalition building in the South, but the Koch Network and other groups poured millions into the 2010 state legislature races in North Carolina. By 2011 the Department of Justice approved a discriminatory redistricting plan that we would later beat in court, but only after it allowed the election of an extreme Republican supermajority.

The reaction to our fusion movement was the waging of an assault on democracy that in many ways anticipated the Republican Party's embrace of MAGA extremism. Nevertheless, we kept on, and in 2013 we launched Moral Mondays, a campaign involving protest at the state legislature every Monday afternoon as well as in the courts, at the ballot box, and in local organizing across the state.

In response to Mie Inouye's reflection on the challenges of building solidarity, I want to share three lessons we learned in the Moral Monday movement—lessons that are hardly new but rather echo the long history of organizing in America's First and Second Reconstructions. After marching from Selma to Montgomery in 1965, Dr. King said that the great fear of the "Southern aristocracy" was that poor whites and poor Blacks would see their common interests and stand in solidarity against plantation capitalism. Moral Mondays helped me to see that we are called to realize that fear—and, in the process, to hopefully transform some of our adversaries into friends. In 2018 we used what we'd learned in Moral Mondays to relaunch the 1968 Poor People's Campaign as a moral fusion movement to defend and expand democracy across the United States. This work is ongoing, and these lessons outline the strategy we are trying to put into practice.

First, solidarity requires a moral framing. People showed up to Moral Mondays because they saw that what was happening to particular people was wrong, not because they understood our adversaries' strategy. In 2013, when the state legislature pushed a monster voter suppression bill, our movement lifted up Ms. Rosanell Eaton, who had memorized the Preamble to the Constitution to pass a Jim Crow voting exam and gone on to register more than four thousand voters but now, in her nineties, would not be able to vote. Mother Eaton, arrested for her role in a Moral Monday protest, told us all it was time to fight together. We used language from our state constitution and our religious traditions to explain why the denial of Ms. Eaton's humanity wasn't an issue of left versus right but right versus wrong. The common commitment to love, mercy, and the good of the whole provides the first basis for solidarity.

Second, solidarity requires explaining how issues interlock. If voter suppression targeted Black women like Ms. Eaton, we also had to show that it impacted poor white people, college students, and women across the board. When we sued to challenge the final voter suppression bill that passed, we developed a legal strategy based on this fusion vision that was successful in overturning the law in federal court. The interlocking didn't stop there; it was equally important that we show how voter suppression was connected to health care access. Because extremists were able to gerrymander a supermajority in the legislature, they could deny half a million North Carolinians health care by refusing Medicaid expansion under the Affordable Care Act. We disaggregated the numbers to show that hundreds of thousands of those low-income people were white and tens of thousands were veterans, and we invited them to join Ms. Eaton on the stage. In the Poor People's Campaign today, we insist that poverty, systemic racism, ecological devastation, the denial of health care, militarism, and the distorted moral narrative of religious nationalism are interlocking injustices undermining the promise of democracy. We cannot work in silos, with different constituencies for each of these issues. We must learn to name our shared pain to recognize that the forces causing harm are the same.

Third, moral fusion is what holds people together. Inouye is right that "social endurance" is the great challenge for any movement. Our adversaries believe they can outlast us; when we protest, they say, "Let them blow off their steam. They'll be gone next week." But from the beginning of Moral Mondays, we insisted that this had to be a movement, not a moment—we were determined to keep showing up. In 2014 over eighty thousand people showed up in the dead of winter to declare, in body, soul, and political engagement, "Forward together, not one step back."

How do we nurture endurance, especially among people often struggling to survive? My understanding of movements is informed by the biblical notion that the stone that the builders rejected becomes the chief cornerstone. In Moral Mondays, the people denied access to Medicaid, the people whose votes were being suppressed, the people who saw how cuts to public education were going to hurt their communities—these were the people who recognized the importance of our moment, and they kept showing up despite threats and major pushback from those in power. People who've lived with their backs against the wall see that kind of resistance as confirmation of their power, and that is why, throughout history, people rejected by society are often the very ones to lead transformative movements. "Only a dying mule kicks the hardest," they used to say in the South African struggle against apartheid.

As I've traveled the United States over the past five years, I've seen that the 140 million poor and low-income people who know this country isn't working for them are the leaders we need to reclaim the promises of democracy and to build a Third Reconstruction. Culture-war tactics are designed to pit us against each other, but poor and low-income people are like the three Hebrew children in the Book of Daniel who knew that, when they faced the fiery furnace, their only hope was to stick together. The biblical text says that, unexplainably, a fourth person emerged to join them in the fire.

For those who don't share the language of faith, a metaphor from the physical world may suffice. Hydrogen and oxygen, on their own, are two of the most volatile elements in nature, but when they come together as H_2O, they form a molecule necessary to all life as we know it. In a similar way, my work over the past two decades has taught me that interest groups can be both powerful and volatile when we work in silos, but when we come together in moral fusion movements, we can become something more than any of us is capable of on our own—maybe even something powerful enough to sustain the promises of democracy and the health of our planetary home.

BLAME NEOLIBERALISM
Daniel Martinez HoSang

THE TWIN pandemics of COVID-19 and police violence in 2020 seemed to augur a new era of solidarity and collective action. In the memorable words of Arundhati Roy, the moment promised "a portal, a gateway between one world and the next." The signs were everywhere: in the street demonstrations that drew those "dying of being alone," as Mie Inouye movingly recounts; in a flourishing of bold experiments in mutual aid; in the provision of public goods, from unemployment insurance to vaccines; perhaps even in the torrent of carefully worded statements from universities, businesses, news organizations, foundations, and other institutions promising to take action against structural injustice.

Yet as Inouye notes—and I share her assessment—the imperative that sent people into the streets and one another's lives on new terms did not produce a "sustained multiracial movement." Her reflections prompt two related questions. What is it, exactly, about political and social life today that makes solidarity seemingly "impossible" to realize? And given these constraints, what can we do to build mass movements—to give large numbers of people the opportunity to practice solidarity?

To be sure, some of the lost promise of 2020 can be attributed to the resurgent power and backlash of the right, but I don't think all of it can. Nor can it be explained by divergent material interests, ideology, or identities. After all, as Inouye suggests, interests are not given; they are made. Political theorist Lisa Beard expands on this idea in her indispensable new book, *If We Were Kin*. "The *we* of politics," she argues, is forged through collective action and shared reflection and consciousness. It is within particular spaces and experiences that "intimate appeals" for identification serve to reconceive "the lines of relationship between self and other." In other words, shared interests, ideology, or identification are the *result* of organizing, not its premise or precondition.

Why, then, did the 2020 mobilizations not themselves produce, in more cases, a bigger sense of "we"? In the sites where we might have expected solidarity to take root and flourish the most—among the students and young people who took to the streets, on college and university campuses, and within many activist, labor, social justice, and nonprofit organizations—it actually imploded. As Working Families Party national director Maurice Mitchell noted in *The Forge* last November, in many cases, the very groups rooted in building solidarity and collective action became engulfed in internal conflicts. These were not just familiar leftist squabbles over strategy, leadership, or organizational culture. (Some degree of strategic debate is routine and ineliminable.) Instead, many community, labor, and social justice groups experienced full-blown eruptions.

I have experienced several of these conflicts firsthand and heard about countless others from friends and colleagues. The stories differ in details, but the broad narrative is largely the same: a focus on making reforms allegedly required to achieve justice within organizations often displaced a focus on organizing for broader transformations in society at large. Indeed, social justice groups at their best promise a respite from the daily degradations of neoliberalism, and perhaps a prefigurative microcosm of the world we want to build. But in this context, goals and orientations drastically shifted: from the structural to the interpersonal, the social to the institutional, and the political to the moral. Feelings of uncertainty, ambivalence, or disorientation—themselves produced by the everyday brutalities of racial capitalism—became expressed through accusations of betrayal, insincerity, and hypocrisy. Calls for organizational discipline in the service of wider movement aims were condemned as excuses for abuse or instruments of top-down control, and demands for "deference" flourished, as Inouye notes. Solidarity, according to this view, is for chumps.

In their book *Insubordinate Spaces: Improvisation and Accompaniment for Social Justice* (2019), Barbara Tomlinson and George Lipsitz argue that far from dismantling the hypercompetitive and retributive culture of neoliberalism, these practices express and reinforce it. "Being hurt can make people want to hurt others," they write:

> Injured individuals and groups see a mirror of their own subordination in the eyes of the people closest to them. They can come to perceive people who might be allies as enemies, to be repulsed by the powerlessness they see around them and in the mirror, and to long for escape from association with those similarly aggrieved and with their problems.

For Tomlinson and Lipsitz, it is the experience of neoliberalism—living under a regime of never-ending competition, loss, and humiliation—that leaves us so ill-prepared for the "conflict, risk, and time" Inouye identifies as the necessary groundwork for enduring solidarity. To counteract these effects, they prescribe "accompaniment"—the "attention, communication, and cooperation" that must be learned and repeatedly practiced to end the cycle of mutual recrimination and lateral punishment.

Inouye is thus right: productive conflict has an essential role to play within organizing and movement building precisely because it fosters collective learning. In a 2020 interview, scholar-activist Ruth Wilson Gilmore made a similar contention about the role that political education must play in forging more capable social movements. "The power of literacy to make us fit for struggle must be exercised like a muscle," she said, "not waved around like a membership card." I thought of Gilmore's metaphor when reading Inouye's reflections on Illinois Black Panther Bob Lee. It takes a lot of practice for most of us to do what he did. That's because organizing and facilitating are hard-earned skills, and like other social skills we exercise when we work together with others, they improve with experience. As Gilmore often says, it's something that her students who are artists and athletes take for granted: you get better, you develop the chops, you exercise the muscles, through relentless practice.

I think any explanation of the political aftermath of the 2020 uprisings is incomplete without this insight. Our movements have not run aground on the shoals of divergent interests, conflicting ideologies, or incommensurable identities; difference alone is not, and never has been, the enemy of solidarity. Rather, we failed to develop more lasting bonds in part because neoliberalism has made us—and here I mean not only the broad landscape of labor, community, and social justice groups but many of us in minoritized fields of study within higher education—insufficiently practiced in the craft of solidarity.

That is not our destiny. As Inouye notes, mass protest is spontaneous and constrained, but that does not mean we cannot "prepare to make the most" of it when it does erupt. To ensure its insurgent energies are directed at the stations of power and domination rather than at one another—to build the "social endurance" Inouye calls for and to make ourselves fit for struggle—we must start practicing now. We must exercise the muscles that neoliberalism atrophies. And we must do so at every opportunity: in our classrooms, in our organizing campaigns, in our reading groups and unions—everywhere there is struggle.

KEEPING GOING
Nathan R. DuFord

SOCIAL ORGANIZATIONS, including political groups, endure through time—some only for short periods, some for generations. Mie Inouye is right to ask how and why they endure, not least because groups too often fail to lay the groundwork to make endurance possible. What leads some organizations to hang together, and what can we learn from them to better maintain those that threaten to fall apart? Conversely, how can we know when it might be the right time to part ways?

Inouye gives two key examples of groups that often endure despite significant conflict, disagreement, or diversity of opinion: family and religious community. We can extract from these examples two elements that promote their persistence through time.

Consider family first. One of the most distinctive features of the family is that most of its members do not choose to be part of it. Families endure precisely because people take the relationship to be involuntary—not really a matter of choice. (Most people today do choose their partners, in some sense, but even this case often entails something one doesn't really choose: having to put up with one's in-laws.) Of course, many people know that you can break these bonds; estrangement is not all that unusual. But it is often an act of last resort: people try to maintain their family relationships even despite abuse, neglect, and harassment.

As for religious affiliations, Inouye notes that it should have been easier for her to leave Mormonism than it was. What makes it difficult to leave a religious community is not unlike what makes it difficult to break ties with one's family. In fact, the two cases are often intertwined: one reason it is often difficult to leave a religion is precisely that it is the religion of one's family. When we are young, both familial relationships and the religious practices embedded in them are involuntary. My parents were conservative evangelicals when I was born, and I was given no choice of religious practice as a child. At some point these things become voluntary, whether in a legal or psychological sense, but even then we may not feel as though we really have a choice to leave. Even in the face of a crisis of faith or a dramatic falling out with family, many try to work through the rift rather than make a decisive break.

This is one way that political organizations can persist despite widespread conflict: a sense of involuntary collectivity. In other words, members can feel they have no choice. Some might feel they are organizing for their life—that their basic survival or livelihood is at stake. Just as we are born into a family or born into a nation (neither of our own choosing), some may feel born into struggle—because they are subjected to domination, exclusion, or oppression, conditions not of their own choosing. Inouye reminds us that the bonds tying us to political organizations or social movements, like those tying us to the family or the church, usually are indeed voluntary: they can be broken, even if we often feel they can't. But until we reach a breaking point, an involuntary sense of duty, obligation, or self-preservation can compel us to keep showing up.

Another factor promoting persistence in Inouye's two key examples is an orientation to the future. While not all religions function to make some future promise in exchange for contemporary suffering, humiliation, and sorrow, many do. Members of religious groups may disagree vigorously about the major tenets of the faith, but they very often share a basic vision of the future. Something similar can be said of families, at least in the contemporary United States. Families project themselves into the future; indeed they cease to exist without reproducing themselves through time—that is, without children. Families are intimately bound up with parenting, child care, and elder care—practices oriented around future plans or future obligations.

This orientation to the future can also generate endurance in political groups and social movements. Such groups are relatively easy to maintain when they are actively succeeding in their goals, gaining momentum toward them, or recruiting many new members. But these moments are rare. Much more frequently, political organizations fail in their main goals; the hard work of the members is not rewarded with success. In such cases, the promise of winning, or building a better future, can compel members to stick together.

Both of these elements—a sense of involuntariness and an orientation to the future—can facilitate endurance through conflict.

But precisely because of that power, they can also have unwelcome effects: making excuses for current bad practices, for example, or promoting resignation to unjust conditions, or deferring action until some perpetually unspecified right time. (Indeed, what's more conservative than insisting on the organizations we have, to the exclusion of others we might build?) Keeping these two elements in balance—a conservatism that enables the organization to persist through time and a radicalism that seeks justice and enables the organization to take risks in order to make change—is fraught with difficulties.

This clash of aims and conflicting motivations need not be destructive: it is part of the work that accepting disagreement can do for an organization. Not all members need to be focused on the future goal; some can be focused on generating prefigurative conditions now. Not all members need to feel an involuntary sense of duty or obligation to the cause; some can, perhaps should, feel freer to walk away. In this sense, Inouye's prescription of shared "ideology" may not be so necessary. Instead, the success of solidarity groups often hinges on the participation of many different types of members, who show up—and stay, when they do—for different reasons.

TRANSCENDING DIFFERENCE
Alex Gourevitch

MIE INOUYE rightly sounds a note of disillusionment regarding the legacy of the 2020 uprisings. With the exception of small numbers of activists and hopeful moments like this summer of strikes in the United States, today's efforts in mass struggle—even on the other side of the largest street protests in U.S. history—pale in comparison to the enormous powers of socialist and communist parties, militant labor unions, and anticolonial movements of the past. Current movements do not generate enduring organizations that integrate local struggles into a social force. To solve this problem, Inouye invites us to forge stronger bonds of solidarity.

But among whom, exactly? One possibility is everyone in our disintegrating society, or even all mankind. After all, over the past few decades, social connections have thinned and kept on thinning; we are far more disconnected than in the 1990s. Inouye seems to have a narrower audience in mind: not all of humanity, nor a national political community, but potential members in a party or political organization.

On this front, there are two quite different groups of potential partisans we might seek to reach, or rather to call into existence, with the language of solidarity. On the one hand, there are those who might be part of a militant minority—people who dedicate themselves wholly and completely to the cause. On the other hand, there are those take time from their normal lives to strike, contribute, vote, march, and hopefully discipline the organization that represents and leads them. There is no emancipatory struggle without both groups, but they are bound by different ties.

The famous slogan "an injury to one is an injury to all" sheds light on the second kind of solidarity, the sort that can hold masses together in common struggle. Now a common phrase on the left, it was first made popular by the Knights of Labor, who emblazoned a version of it on their official logo and successfully united white and Black men and women together in the largest interracial political organization of workers in the nineteenth century. The idea entails a range of actions we associate with solidarity: don't cross the picket line, even if you need the job or goods on the other side; contribute money or time to the strike, even if you had other plans; go out on sympathy strike, even if that comes with a risk to your job, family, or well-being.

What makes these sorts of ties possible? Not just shared "ideology," as Inouye puts it, as shared injury: a specific harm to a person in virtue of their membership in an oppressed group. Injury to any one worker—in the form of dangerous conditions, inadequate pay, or demeaning treatment—is an affront to all who are subject to the power of bosses, for example. The proper response to such injury is the collective exercise of power against collective subjection. That self-emancipatory action creates and reinforces the sense of shared fate and possibility.

Inouye's invocation of ideology points more to the other sort of solidarity: the tighter, closer-knit bonds among the militant minority. An ideologically coherent political party offers its members something more than anything the current left offers: the solidarity of a self-transforming belonging. This is not just the fellow feeling that comes with ordinary membership in a group; it is particular to embattled organizations that make extreme demands on their members and whose aspirations are impractical. The extremity of demand, and knowledge that each is voluntarily submitting to it, play a key role in its special kind of solidarity.

Consider Vivian Gornick's interviews with former members of the Communist Party USA in *The Romance of American Communism* (1977). Gornick observes the seemingly paradoxical fact that disciplined commitment to party life expanded each individual's sense of self. Party life was "one of the most amazing of humanizing processes," she writes: "that process whereby one emerges by merging; whereby one experiences oneself through an idea of the self beyond the self and one becomes free, whole, and separate through the mysterious agency of a disciplining context." Reviewing the recent rerelease of Gornick's book, political theorist Corey Robin observes that the bond of political commitment offers not just unity across difference but a whole new kind of personhood. We become joined to others not just by abstract purpose but a public happiness—"the joy of collective action and the enjoyment of one another."

Yet much in our current culture seems to resist this call for total self-transformation, this "merging" with others. Inouye embraces transformation up to a point; she calls solidarity "the choice to bump up against other people . . . and allow oneself to be changed by the impact." But she also says that the "promise of coalition is that we can work together across difference to change the prevailing social arrangement without fully transcending the ways that it differentiates us and even pits us against each other." Why not transcend difference? World-changing political work is a life-defining activity in which we put aside who we are and live as a professional revolutionary, party member, or comrade, and we do so with others for whom the cause is also life-defining. This commitment isn't just one thing you happen to have in common. It will be the most important thing—a bond that makes all differences trivial.

This sort of solidarity requires more than the "epistemic humility" Inouye prescribes: it means becoming someone else entirely. The new self that emerges is capable of things only because others are also acting with them. Indeed, these new capacities, and therefore oneself, rely heavily on trust in others. When others do their part, the results are thrilling—in part because each trusted each other. This kind of collective achievement is hard to come by, especially in a society as atomized, calculating, and fragmented as ours.

I suspect this helps to explain the perennial debates over "identity politics" on the left. These fights, I think, are ciphers for the problem of trust. Depending on the space, white people, or straight people, or cis people, or white women, or gay men, or whomever are viewed as potentially risky "allies," rarely, if ever, to be fully trusted—perhaps even destined to harm or betray us. Every conversation becomes a test of informal norms of interaction, and violations are all too regularly sharply and publicly punished. The best we get, as a result, is a limited alliance or coalition, constantly policing boundaries that are not to be crossed or dissolved. The effect is that each keeps each other at a strategic arm's length, standing at the intersections of oppression but walking on opposite sides of the road.

The trouble is not just that this form of relation can be joyless but that distrust and uncertainty corrode solidarity. What is left but to retreat back into the very identities that we ought to be transcending? Inouye is right to see a distinctive kind of solidarity at work in religious groups, where people don't just count on each other but overcome their differences. The premise is universal: whatever else you are, whatever your flaws, you are—or at least, can become—one of us. The language of universalism no doubt can hide exclusions in practice, but many religious organizations appear to be doing a better job than contemporary left movements at living up to the ideal.

The left does not need religion, but it could take a page from religion's success in this regard. Following the lead of figures like Karen and Barbara Fields, philosopher Paul Gomberg proposes that we see existing identities as real but alien impositions of an unjust society. If that's right, developing the sort of solidarity we need to change the world may require dispensing with rather than deferring to the identities we have inherited, precisely in order to forge more just and joyful ones. The left will need to ask more so that it can offer more, and to offer more by asking more—perhaps everything—of itself.

ORGANIZING VIRTUES
Astra Taylor & Leah Hunt-Hendrix

THE HEIGHTENED SENSE of political and ecological crisis in the United States has led to a recent revival of interest in the idea of solidarity. Mie Inouye advances this vital conversation with her insightful reflections on collective action, identity, and how people can work together across their differences.

Compared to discussion of concepts like justice, liberty, and equality, the literature on solidarity is remarkably limited. Part of the challenge writers face is defining the term. Those who have studied the concept have offered a range of useful taxonomies, a tendency that goes all the way back to Emile Durkheim's opposition between organic and mechanical solidarity. In recent decades, for example, authors have differentiated between factual and normative solidarity; civic, social, and political solidarity; and mundane and sublime solidarity. In our own forthcoming book, we delineate between what we call transformative solidarity and reactionary solidarity.

As we see it, transformative solidarity involves coming together across differences with the explicit goal of creating democratic social change. Transformative solidarity is both political and personal; it shifts both social structures and the individual, altering how we see ourselves, others, and the wider world. In this way, transformative solidarity reaches out to other people and to new and different futures. By contrast, reactionary solidarity turns in, affirming sameness and the status quo. Where the former expands the circle of inclusion, the latter is defined by and reinforces exclusions.

Neither form of solidarity is a purely spontaneous phenomenon. As anyone who has done political work knows, solidarity must be organized into being, often under incredibly difficult conditions. In our society, transformative solidarity is actively undermined and sabotaged at every turn, from the isolating and competitive nature of capitalism to outright criminalization or violent coups, while its reactionary counterpart is encouraged by vitriolic media and other well-funded institutions on the right. We agree with Inouye on the need to intentionally cultivate transformative solidarity through organizing that counteracts these forces of division.

The identity of "worker," for example, had to be constructed. It was developed over decades during the 1800s, bridging the gaps between various kinds of laborers who didn't think they had much in common but came to see that they did as trade unions grew and spread. This work is necessarily ongoing: divide-and-conquer strategies pull people apart, and it takes hard work to build institutions that can hold us together. Solidarity must be made and remade and remade again.

Both of us have experience building organizations that nurture solidarity and create new active and politically conscious constituencies. Astra is cofounder of the Debt Collective, the country's first debtors' union, which aims to unite multiple kinds of debtors under one big tent. Leah cofounded both the Solidaire Network and Way to Win—donor collaboratives that fund progressive social movements and electoral organizing, respectively. In these contexts, we've witnessed and participated in processes of building collective identities and cultivating ideological orientations that emphasize solidarity over private self-interest and that aim at leveraging structural change.

Consider the Debt Collective. Being a debtor has traditionally been frowned upon and seen as a sign of personal and even moral failure. To confront this obstacle to collective action, the Debt Collective has worked to forge a new "we" by encouraging people to reject the stigma and find connection in shared struggle. The recognition that debt is a systemic condition rather than an individual problem can have a transformative impact on people's self-conception while also opening up new avenues for building working class solidarity and power. As this example suggests, membership organizations play a significant role in the possibility of solidarity—and for democracy as a whole. They have transformative potential because they envelop individuals in new norms and offer them new ways to understand their identities and life circumstances.

For much of the twentieth century, labor unions, neighborhood associations, and other civil society groups—including religious ones, as Inouye recounts—filled this function. But a notable change

Taylor & Hunt-Hendrix

has taken place: in the wake of attacks on organized labor, coupled with changes to the tax code in the early 1900s, nonprofit organizations—both 501(c)3s, which cannot engage in political activity, and 501(c)4s, which can engage in lobbying—have become an increasingly prominent structure for collaboration. While unions still play a hugely important role—indeed, the recent militancy of the Teamsters, Autoworkers, Writers and Actors guilds, and incipient efforts at Starbucks and Amazon suggest a revitalization of labor may be afoot—nonprofits are the primary legal structures through which solidarity work, or its semblance, now takes place.

We join the chorus of those who have sounded the alarm about this development and about the negative influence of philanthropy on social movements more broadly. Thanks to books like *The Revolution Will Not Be Funded* (2017) and Anand Giridharadas's *Winners Take All* (2018), it is now well understood that donors can abuse their power to influence their grantees, whether consciously or not. By drawing on Leah's experience, we think another path is possible—not a complete solution, given the vast structural problem, but at least a model for moving from charity or noblesse oblige to solidarity. What we call philanthropy-in-solidarity involves understanding that you aren't *helping other people*; you are participating in movements that aim to change our social and political structures and ultimately undermine the very conditions that lead to the undemocratic concentration of wealth and power.

Throughout this work, a crucial question is how people from diverse race and class backgrounds can bring their whole selves to solidarity work and navigate the conflicts that may arise. Like Inouye, we believe that conflict is a necessary and inevitable component of solidarity. Solidarity involves defining a "we" that is differentiated from a "them." Workers versus bosses is one classic example. But what about conflict within an organization, or within a group that supposedly has a shared purpose? Can individuals with diverse experiences and interests build real and effective solidarity? Can we have debates and disagreements without tearing each other and our organizations down? How can we resist the domination of some over others in solidarity organizations, while also avoiding the deference politics that often seems to be its alternative?

There is no simple or single answer to these questions, but we believe that membership organizations have a key role to play. They enable the group cohesion and the "social endurance" Inouye calls for, both of which are necessary to overcome obstacles, engage in constructive conflict, and process hard conversations, frustrations, and disappointments.

The Debt Collective once again offers an example. After fighting for student debt cancellation for over a decade and successfully pushing President Biden to announce a plan to deliver up to $430 billion in relief, the cause suffered a major blow when the ultraconservative majority on the Supreme Court struck down Biden's initial plan in June (though other legal avenues remain available to him). This is precisely the kind of backsliding moment when organizations can sink into infighting. The Debt Collective sees its task as communicating a strategy for the fight ahead and providing a forum to help people turn their anger and despair into coordinated action—lest it curdle into cynicism, apathy, or discord.

Taylor & Hunt-Hendrix

In this way, membership organizations transform solidarity from a rallying cry to a way of being together. They do so, in part, by promoting a set of virtues that help us become the kinds of people who can manage and navigate conflict constructively—virtues such as justice, forbearance, humility, curiosity, courage, hospitality, and commitment. These virtues can help us speak to each other honestly, even about difficult subjects and feelings, in ways that others are more likely to hear and receive—while also helping us muster the solidarity, strategy, and determination to engage in meaningful conflicts with the systems and decision makers that are damaging our lives and incinerating the future.

As we understand it, then, solidarity is not synonymous with unity, or even with shared identity, ideology, or goals; it names the bonds that enable us to form and exist in community over time. That time will involve hashing out differences and disagreements, messing up and making amends, making progress and losing ground. We should understand solidarity as both a means and an end, our daily practice and our purpose. Solidarity describes the texture of the democratic community we aspire to create, but just as critically, it is our source of power to get there. Without solidarity, we'll remain divided, which means we're already conquered.

SO MANY ANTINOMIES
David Roediger

AS MIE INOUYE tells us in her frank comments on her own activist persistence, solidarity is a desire that some of us need to practice. Often the satisfactions of common struggles never leave us. If we are lucky, we search for the next fulfillment even decades later. This desire applies to those organizing with people who share their oppression and those who come to witness and support.

Desiring solidarity is mostly a good thing. Sometimes experiencing it is transcendent—like catching the Holy Ghost. Such epiphanies—here Inouye's piece again provides apt guidance and provocation—require thought and caution from those who experience it and want to do organizing ethically and well. Seeing the limits of possibilities also becomes a kind of self-care.

At its best the word "solidarity" gets shouted or sung. We can imagine hearing solid and then air in happy juxtaposition. Indeed, solidarity requires both: digging in and soaring, linking arms, and dreaming together. It looks easy at times, like a slow-motion soccer goal that makes us wonder why such magic does not always happen. And yet, there are plenty of scoreless draws in social movement histories. They can last for years. Movements splinter in ways suggesting that they were less solid than they seemed.

As Inouye grapples with this rhythm in her own life and the lives of her students after the rebellions following George Floyd's murder, she arrives at an almost perfect example of a category of quandaries Immanuel Kant called *antinomies*—contradictory propositions having similarly convincing claims to truth. "Solidarity is an essential component of struggles for justice," she writes, "but on the other hand, actually existing injustice renders it impossible."

I was glad that she announced that dire position and glad she did not stop there, especially now that as a word, at least, solidarity is trending upward. The varied uses of the word have more than compensated for a steep decline in talk of "labor solidarity" from its peak in the early 1960s to 2019: we now talk of solidarity with Palestine, with Standing Rock, with Iranian women, with Ukraine.

Intellectuals have joined in solidarity's proliferation with a flurry of articles and books. Some of the best of those appear in Inouye's account. When I gave an American Studies Association presidential address in 2015 under the title "Making Solidarity Uneasy," the limb I occupied was a lonely one. Following the murders of Trayvon Martin, Mike Brown, and others, just as talk of solidarity was picking up steam in an eruption of protest, I wondered whether solidarity was always a good thing—or whether it instead could be premised on leaving too much, or too many, out. What of those moments when the seeming ease of organizing gives way to harder times? Was solidarity really so easy, however much we desired it? At the time I found little theory to go on from the recent past; most of what I read to prepare for the speech came from the twentieth century. Now we verge on having a subspecialty that could be called "solidarity studies." We get to think about how solidarity is deepened if it is "moralized" and think through the critical implications of how it is "racialized." This important new work was invigorated by activity in the streets: Occupy and especially Black Lives Matter.

In the wake of Brown's death, I sat in—mainly to bring snacks— on a St. Louis meeting planning the details, including chants, for a demonstration reacting to Brown's killing. "Hands up / Don't shoot" had by then emerged as a central slogan. Those chanting it typically raised their own hands with the first two words. The meeting sparked a discussion of whether white marchers should chant and raise hands. Did such street theater claim for whites a danger that in reality fell with deadly consequence primarily on the Black participants, both in demonstrations and daily life? Two positions emerged, by no means predicted by the race of the speakers. One urged that loud, unified chants made protests better. The other accepted as much but argued that the threat of Black "premature death," as Ruth Wilson Gilmore puts it, constituted the very point of the demonstration.

Nobody won the debate, or should have. Marchers made their own choices. The difficulties in deciding flagged another antinomy, or maybe the same one outlined by Inouye. In several cities on a subsequent speaking tour, I brought up the small tactical debate in St. Louis lots, feeling it represented an effort to theorize how solidarity

Roediger

could and should work. In each city activists recalled having a similar exchange, either over that chant or theatre involving "die-ins."

Not surprisingly, the new scholarly interventions regarding solidarity reflect powerfully on race and white advantage. They have helped me to see that I grew up experiencing at least two kinds of solidarity, one named and the other not. My relatives worked as electricians and telephone operators, as well as in quarrying, pipefitting, school teaching, and printing. They overwhelmingly had union jobs and appreciated strike support, from the bringing of a meal to refusing to cross picket lines. Teamsters seemed heroes when they refused to deliver to struck workplaces even to my otherwise very conservative kin. I became a historian of labor in part to ensure that such experiences of collective power were not lost.

But the working-class town where I mostly grew up was also a "sundown" one, devoted to excluding Black people after dark. Even as critical race theory and critical whiteness studies emerged, I would have called that commitment white supremacy, not solidarity. The idea that solidarity could be anything but wonderful struck me as implausible. If it were imperfect, it just needed to expand, with class issues destined to provide a basis for unity in the very longest run. I thought that if sundown townspeople stood on their right to exclude, even as they practiced mutual aid for the included, what they were practicing was not (yet) solidarity.

In his classic work, *The Division of Labor in Society* (1893), sociologist Emile Durkheim insisted that the insularity of traditional society did count as a kind of solidarity. He termed it "mechanical" and found it terrifying. More recently, the late Tyler Stovall's great work of history *White Freedom* (2020) argued that we can't save the ideal of freedom by severing it from its links to racism; in similar fashion, Inouye, Juliet Hooker, and others practicing solidarity studies insist that racialized solidarity—that is, white solidarity—be named and combatted. In its Jim Crow manifestations, solidarity certainly is terrifying, in ways that underline why "expanding the circle" cannot suffice to foster the solidarity that we desire. As anti-apartheid fighters told me decades ago in South Africa, the way to non-racialism is through race. So many antinomies. But as Inouye reminds us, confronting them—working through them—is still our best hope.

POOR ORGANIZING
Liz Theoharis

I WAS EIGHTEEN when I first started organizing in Kensington, on the boundary between lower north and northeast Philadelphia. At the time very racially diverse, the neighborhood was an emblem of the country's changing economy; once an epicenter of the textile industry, it was pummeled by deindustrialization in the 1970s and 1980s, and before the 1996 federal welfare reform law, the two main sources of income for residents were welfare and drugs. A peasant organizer from Haiti told me that the housing and health conditions in mid-1990s Kensington looked as bad as those in her hometown.

Mie Inouye opens her essay with a bracing question: "Why do you organize?" In Kensington, the task of uniting, organizing, and building solidarity among its diverse and impoverished population began at the level of sheer survival. The neighborhood was quietly performing epic feats of ingenuity, often collectivizing scarce resources to provide food, housing, and protection from an antagonistic police force and city government. The Kensington Welfare Rights Union (KWRU)—an outgrowth of efforts of poor women who had organized with the National Welfare Rights Organization (NWRO), the largest poor people's organization of the 1960s—emerged from this street-level activity, and I quickly joined. Over time the group adapted the spontaneous survival tactics people were already using into what we called "projects of survival"—a politicized form of mutual aid designed to meet some of our member's most immediate needs while also fighting for structural changes that could transform the conditions they were living in.

We borrowed the name from the Black Panthers, who in the 1960s and '70s created "survival programs" like free health clinics and a free breakfast program. The Panthers saw these programs as a way to build a movement that could spark larger political change, and they infused all their survival work with deep political study and analysis, highly visible protest, sophisticated communications and cultural organizing, and a commitment to sustaining leaders who could stick and stay for the long haul. All these factors helped build the "endurance" that Inouye rightly points out is critical to a movement's effectiveness.

Building on the work of the Panthers and similar organizing efforts, we established homeless encampments and coordinated housing takeovers across Kensington. We flooded welfare offices, helping community members navigate the byzantine welfare system to access the benefits. As one summer turned into fall and a cold front swept through a large KWRU encampment known as Tent City, we decided to move into a vacant church a few blocks away. Earlier that year the Archdiocese of Philadelphia had shuttered St. Edward's Catholic Church, but some congregants continued to come back every Sunday to pray on the church steps. Eventually dozens of Tent City residents walked up those steps and broke the iron locks on the front doors, igniting a highly publicized occupation that lasted through the winter. Inside, we hung posters and banners; one asked, "Why do we worship a homeless man on Sunday and ignore one on Monday?" We fed and cared for one another in a racially and religiously diverse "congregation" of our own, whose youngest resident was four months old and whose oldest was in his nineties. Our occupation ultimately pressured the Archdiocese to re-prioritize its ministry within poor communities, electrifying the local media and forcing Philadelphians to pay attention to the city's rampant poverty.

In the short term, survival projects like Tent City and the St. Edward's takeover allowed us to build trust within Kensington and meet the needs of community leaders, many of whom were mothers on welfare. These projects also served as bases of operation for bigger and bolder organizing—not just in Kensington, but in alliance with struggles of the poor across the city, state, country, and world. These experiences opened my eyes to a new way of understanding how social change occurs. Amid chaos and catastrophe, poor and oppressed people rarely wait to be saved; they take whatever lifesaving action is available to them, marshaling an immense spirit of cooperation, solidarity, and generosity. This instinct for collective care and survival is the generative ground from which powerful movements from below emerge. By moving into action, poor and oppressed people are able to awaken the indignation and imagination of others, winning wider sections of society and creating a movement that envisions a different kind of political and economic relations.

As we think about building solidarity today, I believe our society still has much to learn from the plight, fight, and insight of its unsung heroines. The welfare mothers of NWRO left a lasting, if underappreciated, mark on the life of our nation. Their position at the very bottom of the economy was painful, but it offered a potent clarity about the immorality and violence of a society that throws out more food than it takes to feed the hungry the world over. As organizer Johnnie Tillmon explained in a groundbreaking 1972 *Ms.* magazine essay:

> I'm a woman. I'm a Black woman. I'm a poor woman. I'm a fat woman. I'm a middle-aged woman. And I'm on welfare. In this country, if you're any one of those things you count less as a human being. If you're all those things, you don't count at all. Except as a statistic.... welfare is a women's issue. For a lot of middle-class women in this country, Women's Liberation is a matter of concern. For women on welfare, it's a matter of survival.

Struggling every day to get by, poor women, especially women of color, depend on an ability to organize communities across lines of historic division. The fusion of their economic, racial, and gender analysis was years ahead of their time, anticipating the notion of intersectionality. Their policy demands were pioneering and prescient—from guaranteed adequate income to universal health care, from affordable housing demands to the right to thrive rather than barely survive. Most importantly, NWRO organizers backed up their visionary analysis with real, robust organization. Long live the visionary leadership and solidarity of welfare rights activists and poor people organizing a movement for change!

DILEMMAS OF SOLIDARITY

Sarah Schulman

SOLIDARITY IS a necessity and a fantasy. Being dominated, punished, blamed, and marginalized by others is often a condition that can only be overturned with the help of third parties. If people could overcome oppression on their/our own, they/we would. Because many cases of oppression are spun as neutral, natural, and not occurring, third-party intervention that reveals the hidden structures and punctures them is often at the center of positive change. It disrupts the agreements that keep inequality secret or justified and ongoing. At the same time, solidarity is an erratic and unpredictable way of life. It can be an excuse for uninformed and misguided actions that create more difficulty for the person or community being assisted. For those in solidarity, it can be unfulfilling, dangerous, and deprive the assister of the protections of their own dominance to the point not where equality is achieved, but where they become unable to have impact.

As a person who offers solidarity and who very much needs solidarity, I know the material difference it makes, how difficult it is to score, and how often it stops short of really delivering. Mie Inouye captures this complexity of solidarity in her reflections on conflict, including the intermixing of personality and substance. Needing concrete help from people who have access is a spotlight on their/our character strengths and flaws, hypocrisies and willingness to risk their/our own security. Being the person offering solidarity is a constant revelation of inadequacies, effectiveness, biases, ability or inability to change, and a stark record of deliberate attempts to work both sides of the street: that is, to equalize the access of those born with less, while not completely sabotaging one's own potential to thrive in a brutally unequal playing field. And both myself on the receiving end, and the people with whom I am in solidarity with, can be angry, petty, victimy, can overstate harm and blame the helper for pain they/we have not caused. Then again there are great friendships of depth that are life-affirming and transforming, created through solidarity that may not solve the central conflict but that enrich people's lives in other ways, while there are also sometimes no personal enhancements. Visible and measurable social change, as a consequence of cooperation, can be achieved in unpredictable, complex ways that are unacknowledgeable and must grant its own recognition and reward.

The key measure of the consequence of solidarity is the question of "tipping point." This goal is based on the assumption that if enough people support in the often elusive but correct way, the endangered person or community's situation would transform. The brutality against them would stop or become less, and the objectified parties would come closer to equality of access and opportunity, to problem solving and autonomy to a degree that changes people's lives for the better. The "tipping point" is the pot of gold, and sometimes arrives partially in a manner that is deceptive, creating opportunity for individuals and not the masses. Or—as we now live—a society can be so retrograde that inequalities tip in the wrong direction and long ongoing crises become even more devastating. The lie that keeps subjugation in place, male or white or Jewish supremacy ideologies, or other false distortions that render outrageous injustice as neutral and normal—sometimes these prove so intractable that seemingly reasonable, credible voices repeat outrages of untruth with the power of institutions and institutions of power.

Another complex sidebar to solidarity is intimacy. Actually forming personal relationships—friendship, coworker, life partner, collaborator— as a consequence of the choice to receive or give solidarity produces all kinds of new dimensions of complexity. Familiarity breeds contempt, *sometimes*. Dealing with personal cruelties, snubs, blame, or unfair acting out from the person you are standing with can be very challenging. It can hurt, especially if you actually care. It can be justified and it can be profoundly unjustified. Being projected onto as a person in solidarity or receiving solidarity can be disorienting and painful, especially if there is a history of real friendship, support, and sharing. These are real relationships, after all, and therefore come with responsibility. As my collaborator Jim Hubbard said about a mutual friend dying of AIDS who made everyone who loved him miserable, "he forgot that we all have responsibilities to each other until we are dead." No one has the right to demand the time and attention of someone just because you are supporting them; cruelty is cruelty and can have damaging consequences on individuals and movements, even if the punch is up.

The question of tipping point is at the center of Palestine solidarity. On one hand I have never experienced any movement that was so welcoming to everyone. From my first exposure in 2009 to now, I have seen a movement whose leaders have welcomed queer people and trans people across the board. It was an esteemed straight Palestinian professor who recommended to me that I organize an LGBT delegation to Palestine. It was a straight male leader of the Palestine Academic and Cultural Boycott of Israel who went on television with me to make a statement in favor of LGBT civil rights in his vision of an autonomous Palestine. Last year I attended a conference organized by openly gay Palestinian professor Sa'ed Atshan at Emory University on Black and Palestine solidarity. Palestinians are always looking for support and, in my experience, are glad to listen in order to find it. When I was faculty advisor to Students for Justice in Palestine (SJP), I was greeted warmly by the father of one of my students, a member of Islamic Jihad, when I joined him in a demonstration in support of his cousin on hunger strike under Israeli custody. He knew that I am queer and Jewish, and I am sure we disagree about a lot of things, but it didn't interfere with our productive and cordial relationship concerning political prisoners.

On the other hand, there is a lot of factionalization—Palestine, like every society, is multidimensional. It is not a monolith. There are a wide range of factions, and I stay out of internal Palestinian politics. It is not my business to participate in Palestinian society building. My job is to work toward the goal of ending U.S. government funding to the Israeli domination and violent suppression of Palestinian autonomy. This means participating in organizations that are anti-Zionist like Jewish

Voice for Peace, a group of eighteen thousand members, for which I serve on the advisory board. It means volunteering as faculty advisor to SJP. It means supporting and observing the Boycott, Divestment, and Sanctions movement.

In the fifteen years since I committed myself to this solidarity, the grassroots movement around the world in support of Palestinian autonomy has grown and grown. SJP is now one of the most common on-campus political organizations in the United States. Young people everywhere increasingly oppose the occupation. Even the U.S. Congress now has a small but vocal Palestine caucus.

And yet the tipping point of change eludes us. The violence grows and grows. The war crimes of the Israeli government are constant and blatant. The lies of the American media are consistent in their hedging and justifications. The mainstream of the government remains locked in myths and baseless loyalties regardless of party. And the large protests in Israel are starkly focused on a concept of "returning" to a democracy that was for Jews only. This is the greatest challenge to solidarity: when no matter how much your movement expands, cooperates, and how righteous and fair your rhetoric and actions combine, you keep losing with no end in sight. This is where we are challenged to grow, to innovate and to stretch. For example, the rise of Palestinian, Muslim, and pro-Palestine members of Congress means that activists need to be more involved in electoral politics. Lobbying by the Palestinian solidarity community becomes more necessary despite its high cost and low return. Resisting university attacks on people who speak out against Israeli aggression falls to small legal entities like Palestine Legal and the Center for Constitutional Rights, who need our support. Not being afraid to speak up for Palestine, even when being falsely accused of anti-Semitism with consequences for employment, is an act of courage. These concrete actions become more and more important as the grassroots swell and the apparatus ignores. Yes, there is a politics of repetition when it comes to fighting the obvious, but the Palestine solidarity movement has proven to be a courageous and inventive one, whose eye is clearly on the forces that originate the oppression.

There is no easy interpretation and the road to giving and asking for solidarity is filled with minefields and reassessments. Yet, in America at least, nothing—absolutely nothing—advances without coalition. And coalition, also, is filled with images constructed by marketed falsehood. Coalitions are not Benetton ads, *one of you and one of you and one of you.* They are not perfect rainbow structures of integration. Coalitions more often are different constituencies coming together at different moments when their resources and energies can resonate together to create a simultaneity of response more powerful than the contested parties would be able to achieve on their own. These formations are always shifting and are almost never static or without tension. Yet coalitions are the only structure that impacts the larger apparatus. The ideal of the heroic white male individual who arrives to save the day is not only inaccurate, it is actually impossible. It is the cumulative simultaneity of solidarity that creates the paradigm shift so many of us look toward in order to fully live, together, as ourselves.

SETTLE YOUR QUARRELS

Charisse Burden-Stelly

THE WORD "love" does not appear in Mie Inouye's reflections on the meaning of solidarity, but consider these words of Che Guevara in 1965:

> At the risk of seeming ridiculous, let me say that the true revolutionary is guided by great feelings of love. It is impossible to think of a genuine revolutionary lacking this quality. . . . We must strive every day so that this love of living humanity is transformed into actual deeds, into acts that serve as examples, as a moving force.

For Guevara and other twentieth-century revolutionaries, solidarity was an act of love, understood not as eros, agape, philia, or storge but rather as radical responsibility: an unyielding commitment to eradicating the inhumane, forged in political insurgency.

Inouye offers a different perspective. For her, solidarity consists in the ability of comrades—many unsure of their reasons for showing up—to dislike or even hate each other even as they work toward a common end. In this vision, the focus is on belonging and belief (what she understands as "ideology"), not collective action and political struggle. We are invited not to love, nor to find the courage of radical commitment, but to be humble and to embrace dissent.

I think Inouye arrives at this solution because she misidentifies the problem. She has two main targets. First is the compromised form of solidarity the Mormon church offered her family in the wake of their internment, based on the willingness of a comparatively powerful and established entity to charitably include a dispossessed group and the alacrity of the beleaguered to assimilate to the status quo. Second is what philosopher Olúfẹ́mi Táíwò calls "deference politics"—uncritical genuflection to a particular group based on their standpoint and experience of oppression. The two examples are related: deference to the supposed expertise of the oppressed, like "solidarity" based on top-down inclusion and bottom-up compliance with reigning ideology, demands uncritical unity. By engaging Nathan Duford's work and Fred Moten's interpretation of the original Rainbow Coalition, Inouye proposes that we embrace productive conflict and the ability to "express our frustrations, disagreements, and anger with the intent of moving toward a shared goal."

Unlike Inouye, I do not think that demands for unity are the most pressing obstacle to solidarity. What solidarity tends to back is *active commitment*—that is, collective action and concrete objectives to the end of structural transformation. This is the essence of love as radical responsibility. In this way, unity—not as uncritical acquiesce, but as the willingness to struggle together toward a common liberatory end—will play an inevitable and essential role alongside conflict and debate in collective action.

Burden-Stelly

I have identified this form of solidarity in a range of contexts: organizations such as the Sojourners for Truth and Justice, founded by radical Black women to challenge anti-Black state repression and the Korean War, and the Council on African Affairs, a collective aimed at eradicating colonialism and imperialism in Africa; campaigns like those to exonerate W. E. B. Du Bois and the Peace Information Center, who were indicted as agents of a foreign power because of their peace work, and to circulate the *We Charge Genocide* petition, submitted to the United Nations in 1951, accusing the United States of the genocide of African Americans under the UN's own definition; and grassroots challenges to state repression, from the Smith Act of 1940 to the McCarran Act of 1950, which aimed at severely curtailing the civil rights and liberties of political minorities—especially members of the Communist Party—and under which Claudia Jones was deported from the United States in 1955. All these examples exhibit a kind of radical unity and collective responsibility in action.

Running through all these examples is what I have called "mutual comradeship," a set of anticapitalist and antiracist practices developed by radical African descendants in struggles on behalf of the racialized, colonized, and oppressed—and in the face of protracted antiradical state repression. Its foundations are collaboration, reciprocal care, and learning in community rooted in organizing, movement building, collective self-defense, and guerilla scholarship—what Walter Rodney describes as knowledge work rooted in the exigencies of movements and peoples' struggles. As an expression of love as radical responsibility, mutual comradeship guides activism and organizing in the Black radical tradition and helps to bridge strategic unity and productive conflict. It does all this in specifically political circumstances, with a specific political goal: the process of envisioning and striving to build a world beyond racial capitalism and imperialism—and of weathering the inevitable backlash for doing so.

Moving beyond shared ideology, mutual comradeship is simultaneously an ethical, epistemological, and political practice of solidarity. Ethically, it emanates from the guiding principle of courage—the willingness to place oneself at risk for the betterment of others and shared values of cooperative social activity, a common conception of social transformation rooted in the eradication of racial capitalism, and the establishment and maintenance of expectations and standards through consistent struggle, debate, criticism, and self-criticism. These ethics are in the service of protecting, preserving, and valuing not only movements and organizations, but also each other.

Mutual comradeship also constitutes what the late philosopher Charles Mills calls an "alternative epistemology" whereby those in subordinated groups develop critical perspectives on the social system. The epistemological practice of mutual comradeship overcomes the illusory perceptions of hegemonic groups through the difficult work of challenging structural oppression and combating the antagonistic relations it promotes even among fellow travelers. This practice also illuminates and clarifies relations of subjection and presents a liberating vision of society to cultivate a shared understanding of what is to be done.

In terms of politics—the means by which we contest and vie for power, resources, and the ability to collectively organize our lives on our own terms—mutual comradeship employs activism, organizing, movement building, and institution making to cultivate solidarity against the hegemony of racial capitalism. The ultimate aim is to overthrow the existing order to forge peaceful and humanizing social relations—locally, nationally, and internationally. Mutual comradeship also entails what we might call practices of "legacy maintenance"—including archiving, commemoration, public remembrance, and truth telling—predicated upon the enduring commitment to, advocacy for, and protection of those who are erased, obscured, or silenced from popular memory. These practices keep past, present, and future in active dialogue.

Two complimentary expressions of mutual comradeship are particularly germane to our current moment. Audre Lorde advised in *Sister Outsider* (1984) that "unless one lives and loves in the trenches it is difficult to remember that the war against dehumanization is ceaseless." Lorde elucidates that living and loving *in struggle* is the basis of reaching a common understanding all that crushes our humanity—and of relentlessly combatting it. But, as the Combahee River Collective described in 1977, our ability to wage political battle is inextricable from love of self and community. "We realize that the only people who care enough about us to work consistently for our liberation are us," they wrote. "Our politics evolve from a healthy love for ourselves, our sisters and our community which allows us to continue our struggle and work."

It is perhaps George Jackson, though, who spoke most urgently about revolutionary action as radical responsibility to the people, present and future, and as a crucible for the cultivation of love. "Settle your quarrels," he insisted. "Come together, understand the reality of our situation, understand that fascism is already here, that people are already dying who could be saved, that generations more will die or live poor butchered half-lives if you fail to act." If solidarity is the means by which we can and must confront the dire economic, political, and ecological challenges of our moment, then our historical task is as Jackson put it: to "do what must be done, discover your humanity and your love in revolution."

ENDURING SOLIDARITY
Mie Inouye

I BEGAN my essay by outlining what David Roediger helpfully names an "antinomy" of solidarity. On the one hand, solidarity is an essential component of struggles for justice, but on the other hand, actually existing injustice seems to render it impossible. Other antinomies have emerged from the responses. Sarah Schulman notes that oppressed people often need the help of a third party to overturn their oppression, but that third parties can create "more difficulty for the person or community being assisted." Nathan DuFord identifies an antinomy of endurance: in order for organizations to endure, they need a certain conservatism, but that same conservatism can thwart the radicalism that enables organizations to take risks in order to make change—both internally and in the world. And Alex Gourevitch points to an antinomy of transformation: in order to counter the domination that structures our society, we need capacities and self-understandings that domination makes it difficult for us to develop.

As I see it, any process of making a new world from within the old is inevitably accompanied by these and other seemingly unresolvable paradoxes. And yet, organizers find resolutions all the time, even if only provisionally. I think this forum has succeeded at two politically useful tasks of political theory: it has clarified the antinomies that attend the practice of solidarity so that we, as organizers, can better understand why we struggle—and often fail—in the ways that we do, and it has pointed toward some practical resolutions.

As Astra Taylor and Leah Hunt-Hendrix note, and as the range of responses demonstrates, "solidarity" has many meanings. Jodi Dean suggests that my understanding of solidarity is "social" rather than "political." I think this is in part because I (implicitly) define solidarity simply as collective action in pursuit of shared goals. This definition captures the activity of Mormons as well as the members of the old Communist Party that Dean and Gourevitch reference. With Taylor, Hunt-Hendrix, Roediger, and DuFord, I find it useful to define solidarity broadly—not only as a practice of the left—in order to see the (sometimes unexpected) similarities and differences between the activities of collectives oriented toward very different goals. The kind of solidarity that I aim to cultivate in my own organizing is oriented toward a vision of socialism, but many forms of solidarity are not so oriented. As Roediger notes, some are even reactionary.

Admittedly, my essay does attempt to blur the boundaries between the social and the political. As a result, Dean and Burden-Stelly both read me as saying that solidarity is about "the social texture of community" or "belonging" rather than politics and struggle. In fact, I think that solidarity is often social and political at once, even though the people who act in solidarity with each other do not always understand their actions this way. Mormons do not understand the Mormon Church to be a political organization, but I would argue that it is, insofar as it engages (sometimes very influentially) in struggles over the distribution of power and resources in society. Similarly, many leftists reject the possibility that a desire for belonging or collectivity might be driving their political activity. My purpose in exploring my own multiple and simultaneous motivations for organizing was to suggest that, if we are honest with ourselves, the very real human desire for collectivity—a desire that Dean herself writes about powerfully in her works on the party and comradeship—is a big part of what drives most of us to organize. The experience of injury and the need to survive, as Gourevitch, Reverend William Barber II, and Reverend Liz Theoharis powerfully illustrate through historical and contemporary examples, is a potent motivation. But not everyone who is injured decides to organize. It is often a need for sociality that draws people into organizing, at least in the beginning. We should acknowledge this desire—so often denied by neoliberal capitalism—and find ways to help people to satisfy it, rather than disavowing it.

Another reason I emphasize the social dimension of solidarity is that, like HoSang and Gourevitch, I think neoliberalism's four-decade-long erosion of society has decimated the organizational infrastructure and social capacities on which radicals of past generations could draw. Communist organizers like William Z. Foster turned to mainstream labor unions, churches, and fraternal organizations to connect the party to a mass base. Such organizations have since dramatically declined, making the task of organizing the working class much more challenging today. As HoSang notes, neoliberalism has also atrophied the "muscles" we need in order to organize. Jakobi Williams recounts that Bob Lee honed his organizing skills by observing activists in his mother's nightclub, his father's civil rights organizing, and the labor organizing of longshoremen at the union hall across the street from his childhood home. Today there are few Bob Lees among us. We suffer from atomization, individualism, competitiveness, social anxiety, and a lack of resilience to conflict—not only over identity but over anything. It is these effects of neoliberalism (not excessive uncritical unity, as Burden-Stelly suggests) that I take to be the central obstacle to building solidarity in our time.

In response to this obstacle, I suggest that we cultivate social endurance: the capacity to show up to meetings and work together, even when we don't know what kind of conflict lies in store for us, and even when we do not particularly like the other people in the room. Political endurance, which we might define as the capacity to maintain fidelity to a shared political project, is also crucial. But I think social endurance is distinct from and, in some cases, a prerequisite to political endurance, precisely because ideological clarity and commitment often follow from sustained collective practice. I agree with Juliet Hooker that the Movement for Black Lives accomplished important ideological work in articulating a vision of a world in which Black people and all people could thrive, and that the current upsurge in labor organizing contributes to that vision. But on my view, we cannot cohere or disseminate a "conception of the world" without sustained organizing that connects it with practice. Similarly, a long-term commitment to struggle does not usually follow from an intellectual commitment to a cause. Rather, as HoSang also notes, organizing helps us to understand what we are fighting for and why it matters.

I also suggest epistemic humility as an alternative practical application of the insights of standpoint theory to deference politics. Dean glosses both social endurance and epistemic humility as "DEI best practices." I disagree with this characterization. DEI emphasizes deference and conflict avoidance in service of diversifying capitalist institutions and insulating them from liability, while social endurance and epistemic humility are tactics for building the collective capacity to transform those institutions. But I accept Dean's suggestion that these practices are not only tactics; they are also "ethics." With Taylor and Hunt-Hendrix, I see the cultivation of a certain set of virtues, chief among them humility, kindness, and the capacity to endure and learn from conflict, as essential to holding people together for any length of time in our fragmented society and to navigating the inevitable strategic disagreements that Hooker describes, and I am never sure why some leftists recoil from the language of ethics.

Finally, what is the role of conflict and unity in the process of transformation that is necessary to solidarity? Burden-Stelly suggests that I want more conflict on the left and that I think people can and should hate their comrades. That is not my view. Rather, I think that we need to develop the capacity to endure the many kinds of conflict that inevitably emerge through the process of organizing. I appreciate and accept Burden-Stelly's suggestion that love is essential to world-transforming solidarity. On my view, comradely love is not compatible with hatred, but it is compatible with conflict and with disliking each other. We can love our comrades without liking them. We can be comrades without being friends.

In response to my discussion of coalition, a form of solidarity that does not require that we fully transcend the ways the prevailing social arrangement differentiates us, Gourevitch asks, "Why not transcend difference?" Whether or not we see transcending difference as the horizon of socialist organizing, that is not where we are. So how do we organize now, in the transition? My point in turning to coalition is not that we should avoid unity, but that coalition is a way to pursue unity through collective action across real lines of existing difference.

This forum has focused on external conflict: conflict among comrades or potential comrades. But for many of us, the antinomies of solidarity entail sustained internal conflict, too. We are constantly making adjustments to our strategic assessments and organizing practices in order to keep the essential and sometimes nearly contradictory imperatives of solidarity in balance. This is a feature, not a bug, of organizing for a just world under present conditions. In the words of the late Mike Davis, "Moral dilemmas and hard choices come with the turf and they cannot be evaded with 'correct lines.'" Our positions must be "constantly reassessed and calibrated to the conjuncture." As DuFord writes, this effort is "fraught with difficulties." For this reason, developing the capacity to sustain not just external but internal conflict is another crucial form of endurance for leftist organizers to cultivate—one that can make us more responsive to the present situation and to each other, even as we grow more committed to the socialist horizon. ◆

UNION WITHOUT UNANIMITY
Ege Yumuşak

FEW OF US have a voice in the political systems we are embedded in; the decisions that shape our lives are mostly made behind closed doors in rooms we can't access. In theory, one exception to this rule is collective bargaining—a right that only 10 percent of U.S. workers exercise.

The goal of collective bargaining is clear enough: to escape what philosopher Elizabeth Anderson calls "private government," the subjection of workers to the unaccountable authority of employers. By engaging in bargaining, the idea goes, workers can limit the scope of their employer's control over their lives, improve their pay and benefits, and win protections to ensure they are treated with respect and dignity. In their recent book, *Rules to Win By: Power and Participation in Union Negotiations*, veteran labor organizer Jane McAlevey and researcher Abby Lawlor expose how the practice of collective bargaining has often fallen short of this ideal. "Most negotiations today function a bit like our mangled democracy," they argue. Union members may get to elect leaders and bargaining teams, but they rarely "experience the actual process of collective negotiations over the issues that are crucial, urgent, and relevant to their own lives." Instead, they "are told that their role . . . is to vote to ratify or reject a contract presented to them at the end of lengthy, opaque contract negotiations" executed by union management and their lawyers. McAlevey and Lawlor want to empower workers to be more engaged and to change the script unions have long followed at the bargaining table.

The book arrives at the right time. Union election petitions shot up 53 percent from 2021 to 2022, and public opinion polling puts U.S. union support at its highest since 1965, with Americans now viewing unions more favorably than Joe Biden by almost two to one. Just as many workers are getting their first taste of organizing, McAlevey and Lawlor distill crucial insights from six case studies of recent union successes, offering vital prescriptions for making negotiations more democratic while building power vis-à-vis employers. Their central claim—that "high participation" is strategically effective—gives the lie to the supposed necessity of closed, backdoor dealmaking for achieving a win. They call their vision "maximalist," and they see "the democratization of unions" as a "crucial goal . . . urgently needed around the globe."

Given this argument, however, it is striking that many of the book's examples of participation are fairly limited, often leaving little room for serious debate on strategy and in some cases amounting to little more than spectatorship. This tension raises a question: Is democracy intrinsically valuable as a form of worker dignity and empowerment, or is it primarily a means to an end—valuable only to the extent that it advances what union leadership takes to be a "win"? Many rank-and-file workers are offering their own answers in the spirit of *Rules to Win By*'s radical call, demanding new forms of bottom-up agency and rejecting the tendency to see dissent as an obstacle to worker empowerment.

THE CHARGES that McAlevey and Lawlor level at union "position holders" are damning. Top union officials have gotten "too cozy with top bosses," they write, and the default approach of "top-down, backroom, low-participation" negotiations has gone "stale." Unions not only fail to win contracts that workers need to work with dignity; they discourage workers from pushing for more. "The political theorist Robert Michels warned us over a century ago," the authors observe, "that unions, political parties, and all organizations made up of everyday people have to build in guard rails against reproducing hierarchies."

On this score, the book mentions the "sad and enraging story" of the United Auto Workers (UAW), which has long been plagued by leadership and corruption scandals, as "only the most recent example of what mass union democracy can help preempt." In early March this year, just weeks before *Rules to Win By* was published, UAW saw its first direct election of leadership in the union's eighty-eight-year history, ending what critics call the "one-party" control that had prevailed for decades. Reformers won a majority on the executive board, and the union's new president, Shawn Fain, recently vowed to end backdoor negotiations.

McAlevey and Lawlor also take aim at negotiation experts. As they see it, neither of the best-selling primers—William Ury and Roger Fisher's *Getting to Yes* (1981) and Chris Voss's *Never Split the Difference* (2016)—contain actionable advice for union negotiations teams. The former contends that identifying common interests of workers and management can lead to a win-win, but the presumption that "the employer is not only willing to settle but is willing to allow the other party to continue to exist" simply doesn't hold today; now employers are "bent on an ideological crusade to wipe out unions altogether." Voss's prescription of "tactical empathy"—developed in the context of hostage negotiations—does not suit labor struggles either, since employers are as unlikely respond to emotional manipulation as to cooperative compromise. Rather than indulge the pretense of good faith, McAlevey and Lawlor argue, unions should do as employers do: pretend to negotiate but in reality exercise their power. And "to build maximum power, every single step of the negotiating process" must involve "intentional, mass participation."

Rules to Win By thus defends three core tenets of union negotiations: they must be "transparent, big, and open." Negotiations are transparent when negotiators do not sign ground rules that prevent who can be in the room, what can be negotiated, and what can be communicated with people outside the room; the ideal is to relay every update from the bargaining table back to the workers. Negotiations are big when every kind of worker finds voice via an elected representative in every session, even if that requires larger-than-conventional bargaining committees. Finally, negotiations are open when every stakeholder—including every worker covered by the collective bargaining agreement and sometimes community members affected by the business—can attend negotiations as observers.

To realize these three core tenets, McAlevey and Lawlor argue, unions ought to follow twenty strategic principles regarding negotiations. Among them are recommendations about how to submit the union's request for information to the employer and how to prepare the bargaining team for a presentation of demands on the first day of bargaining. Having a detailed information request and sharing the resulting information helps build power, they argue, because it "helps inform workers of the larger pictures they're negotiating within." Similarly, asking workers to plan the first session and including trusted workers from the shop floor "can get negotiations off to a roaring start" because it signals to the management that workers are "in control of the negotiations." These rules are not about how to negotiate particular articles in a contract. Rather, they are "tools that transform a union from low participation to high participation by way of contract negotiations."

THE SIX case studies in *Rules to Win By* are offered as proofs of concept. Perhaps the most thrilling occurs at Pennsylvania's Albert Einstein Medical Center, where McAlevey was hired as a consultant and lead negotiator by the Pennsylvania Association of Staff Nurses and Allied Professionals (PASNAP) union. The book gives a page-turner account of PASNAP's campaign, complete with a months-long legal battle at the National Labor Relations Board (NLRB), additional staff flying in at McAlevey's request from the British Columbia Federation of Labor, and a dramatic strike vote. The nurses participate in high numbers throughout the process. They chart social and economic relationships in their workplaces, have many one-on-one conversations, contact their political leaders and faith-based leaders to get endorsements, don't let a moment go idle—and they reach an agreement within six months.

The win is compelling, but it is not always clear whether high participation is the decisive factor that leads to success in the book's examples. Indeed, many of the cases involve departures from the twenty basic principles, and other factors evidently play a significant causal role. Given the book's largely instrumental account of participation—the suggestion that worker involvement matters to the extent that it helps to build power and thus achieve a "win"—a reader might take these nuances as reasons to reject even the kind of participation that McAlevey and Lawlor call for.

In PASNAP's case, for example, the campaign abandoned bigness and openness by allowing two people—McAlevey and the union's executive director—to negotiate a framework agreement for the timeline of the bargaining process. (In an effort to be transparent, the two leaders do call two workers to outline the deal and allow them to make some calls before accepting the schedule.) The campaign also risked McAlevey and Lawlor's principle that 90 percent of workers should vote for a strike threat in order for it to be credible, as the vote was held without due notice and only over four days. McAlevey and Lawlor report that of the PASNAP nurses who voted, 90 percent moved to strike, but they do not mention how many people voted out of all 925 workers represented by the union. And while the book omits the terms of the Einstein contract, McAlevey and Lawlor disclose at least one tragic concession: in order to get the agreement, PASNAP signed a temporary agreement not to organize three new hospitals in the Einstein network, effectively depriving hundreds if not thousands of other nurses of the right to collective bargaining.

Despite these limitations, I found the PASNAP campaign remarkable in the nurses' ability to keep marching past tough decisions. They applied the rules to win by selectively and at the right time. Indeed, case after case in the book demonstrates the need for improvisation, creativity, and the savvy use of luck. The nurses pushed Einstein to come to the bargaining table by threatening to picket the 2016 Democratic National Convention in Philadelphia after they learned that it would take place on the same day as Einstein's deadline to appeal the recognition of the union. "What a gift," the authors write.

In fact, Einstein nurses could count on another gift: favorable objective conditions. At the time of the campaign, Einstein was desperately trying to recruit more nurses, and a national nursing shortage helped to empower them. In their case, management proved willing to concede even before nurses set a strike deadline, but others haven't been as lucky, as nurses at St. Vincent Hospital in Worcester, Massachusetts, can attest. Organizing with the Massachusetts Nurses Association, they saw a bitter fight, including a ten-month strike.

When workers' resilience is being tested, making space for creativity and seizing lucky opportunities can go a long way, but in one of the book's cases featuring an extremely intransigent employer, a crucial move by political leaders helps to close the deal. Teachers and other certified staff at Mercer County Special Services Educational and Therapeutic Association (MCSSETA) find their way into high-powered negotiations after field representatives from their parent union, the New Jersey Education Association (NJEA), attend a training led by McAlevey and encourage the locals to open up negotiations to members. MCSSETA follows their advice: eighty-six members fill the first session at the school library, and further sessions had to be scheduled in the school gym with as many as 150 members attending.

But even with this early success, MCSSETA negotiators bargain for nearly two years and reach a deal only with luck and after straying from the rulebook. "NJEA president Marie Blistan made a call to . . . Democratic governor Phil Murphy," McAlevey and Lawlor relate, and soon thereafter Blistan met with the county executive who appointed the school board. "A week later, MCSSETA members had the deal they needed." Union members initially veto any closed sessions but change their minds after Blistan's meeting. Behind closed doors, MCSSETA's president gets a major concession on salary increases, which leads to a successful ratification vote involving around one hundred of the union's nearly four hundred members. But the example doesn't offer an analysis of what to do when participation hits a ceiling. When political allies don't come through, and employers remain intransigent, how can workers keep the fight alive?

In their closing chapter, McAlevey and Lawlor acknowledge that their rules aren't meant to be hard and fast; some degree of improvisation—judgment about when and how to apply the principles—is inevitable under varying conditions. "The twenty elements of high-participation negotiations function like key ingredients in a successful recipe," they write: "the amounts might, in a pinch, vary or be substituted for something very similar, but the basic items and the steps do matter." They stop short, however, of giving a systematic framework to discern under what objective conditions these tactics can be applied (or need to be abandoned)—and to make these decisions democratically.

THIS OMISSION POINTS to a subtle tension in the argument of *Rules to Win By*: the distinction between participation and worker empowerment. Workers should participate, the authors argue, by doing things like identifying "potential intersections between their own lives and relationships in the community and key actors and institutions in the power structure," writing articles in article committees, running for a seat in large voluntary bargaining teams, and participating in polls about what to do in the bargaining room. One criticism of tactics in the broad catalog of McAlevey's model has been that they serve a strategy predetermined by professional staff; the authors do not discuss how unions can develop more democratic ways of setting strategy and working through deep disagreement. According to *Rules to Win By*, "a debate or issue that is emerging among workers in the room can be quickly resolved" by caucusing—taking a formal break in negotiations. McAlevey and Lawlor don't address the possibility that debate might not be resolved, especially not quickly.

Given the emphasis on quick resolutions, readers may draw the conclusion that serious dissent should be frowned upon for the sake of the win. Similarly, the authors write:

> When workers who have low trust in their own organization—as many do in today's typical do-nothing-or-do-too-little unions—are invited to take part in the very process at the heart of every union, they can quickly shift to having immense trust in and effective ownership of the organization. This can happen during one negotiation session, if not just one hour in a session, when the union goes out of its way to ensure that all workers understand the process and dynamics of negotiations. . . The old union saying that "The boss is the best organizer" comes to life when workers can witness, firsthand, management lawyers resolutely rejecting reasonable demands, leading skeptical workers to come to the conclusion that their active participation in a collective project is the only way to win changes that meet their pressing needs.

This sort of openness would go a long way to building trust, and it's certainly a far cry from the closed-room, top-down practices that McAlevey and Lawlor reject. But understanding and witnessing the process—even taking part in research or planning activities that help negotiators and other leadership—is not the same as exercising agency over it.

I have seen these tensions in my own organizing experience. I came into the labor movement in 2018 as a graduate student and rank-and-file organizer at Harvard University. At the time, student workers were fighting to set aside a contested 2016 vote over union-izing that was conducted under gross misconduct by the Harvard administration. The NLRB invalidated the results and ordered a new election, but Harvard appealed; it was not until January 2018 that we were guaranteed a second chance.

Worker initiative and situated knowledge came to the fore in seizing favorable conditions. As we headed to a new election, *The Chronicle of Higher Education* exposed decades of sexual harassment by Jorge Domínguez, a professor in Harvard's government department. The lack of real recourse for harassment was already an issue motivating students to join the union effort and something we were organizing around. Even though university administrators moved with lighting speed to force Domínguez into retirement, something had changed: we had a real opportunity to build momentum on the heels of #MeToo. We had already made inroads organizing around Trump's Muslim ban, and we pivoted to use this moment to grow our support even more. We ran a campaign centering immigrants and survivors of harassment and discrimination, and led by our international student and feminist caucuses, we won our union—the Harvard Graduate Students Union (HGSU), a UAW local—in April.

Later that fall, as HGSU headed to its first contract negotiations, I was elected as a representative. Student across campus were excited and agitated, but when we brought up open bargaining, our UAW advisors told us that it would be a great way to put pressure on Harvard, but only if turnout was sufficiently high. While for McAlevey and Lawlor every stage of the negotiation process can be turned into a tactic for power building, our advisors appeared to consider openness optional, primarily of instrumental value. In the end, both arguments see participation as a means to power rather than a matter of principle.

In some contexts, worries over low turnout have become moot. In New York and California, UAW leaders are keen to open the doors of the bargaining room to all because they can count on workers, especially in higher education, to show up. Still, those who attend are often expected to act as spectators. When forty-eight thousand workers at the University of California (McAlevey and Lawlor among them) ended the largest academic strike in history last year without winning any core demands, Michael Paul Berlin argued in *Jewish Currents* that despite practicing transparent, big, open negotiations (in the sense that rank and file were engaged as spectators), union leadership displayed a tendency to "manage, rather than further, the demands coming from rank-and-file workers." The elected bargaining teams had initially championed the demand for a cost-of-living salary adjustment—the most energizing demand for the rank and file—but a narrow majority proved willing to give it up, and a significantly weaker contract was ratified when put to the whole union membership, even after a vigorous "no" campaign.

Deeper union democracy than *Rules to Win By* envisions—more space for debate and meaningful strategic input from the rank and file—might not always lead to outcomes that satisfy all workers, of course. But it is hard to see on what principled basis such opportunities should be ruled out. On the contrary, there are clear risks to denying them: it can reinforce the very anti-democratic tendencies that McAlevey and Lawlor rightfully decry. The principles in *Rules to Win By* don't rule out hierarchical forms of "high participation" at the hands of undemocratic leadership. In the book's paradigm, the role of some workers in negotiations is limited to introducing "efficiencies by enabling real-time fact-checking of management's claims." In the worst case, overly bureaucratic unions may weaponize weak forms of participation to give the illusion of greater democracy and worker empowerment. "It's not too hard to imagine top-down unions trying to legitimize unpopular decisions by saying we had 'open bargaining' so we did everything right," Brandon Mancilla, the newly elected regional director in UAW's Region 9A told me in an interview. "Open bargaining is not a spectator sport. We need to make sure that our contract fights open up possibilities for workers to be involved and take ownership over the campaign beyond watching bargaining."

Mancilla reflects labor's new efforts to increase participation by democratizing union governance. From the Chicago Teachers' Caucus of Rank-and-file Educators and the Union Power caucus of the United Teachers Union Los Angeles to the Teamsters for a Democratic Union and UAW's own Unite All Workers for Democracy, reform caucuses have installed new leadership and are working to make significant changes to culture and practice. Inspired by Kellogg's and John Deere workers who voted down tentative agreements and later achieved transformative contracts, other UAW unions—not just at the University of California—have seen rank-and-file no-vote campaigns over the last two years. Meanwhile, UPS Teamsters have built an app to send out bargaining updates to all workers during ongoing contract negotiations, and they are inviting a number of rank-and-file workers into the bargaining room. All these developments—embodying the call for high participation in *Rules to Win By*—have emerged from rank-and-file militancy, and they point the way to building a more democratic culture of dissent and debate within unions themselves.

Perhaps the most entrenched idea labor has to unlearn is the presumption that union means unanimity. In a recent piece in *Labor Notes*, Helena Worthen and Joe Berry set out to dispel the myth that disagreement among workers necessarily weakens the union. "Far from sending a message to the boss that the union is divided and vulnerable," they write, "a vote no campaign can be viewed as a sign of strength." In their report from a strike at Rutgers in April earlier this year, Bryan Sacks (vice president of the adjuncts' union) and Michael Beyea Reagan (a rank-and-file worker) wrote about decision making near the end of negotiations. "A sizable minority within the union's governing bodies believed the strike was suspended at a time when the unions retained power to press for greater gains," they observe. "They called for a delay in signing the framework to further discuss the matter over the weekend." Their call wasn't heeded, and the strike still won impressive raises and groundbreaking job security provisions for adjunct faculty, but Sacks and Reagan raise reservations about whether this game-time decision was the right one, encouraging open debate about it.

This attitude has long been the exception in the labor movement. More often, the pressure is to reserve conflict and contestation for fights with management. For big, open, transparent negotiations to be a source of strength, a democratic culture and substantial rank-and-file input even in strategic decision making are essential, and achieving them requires seeing conflict not as an obstacle to winning but rather a crucial form of worker agency and political education. In the hands of democratic union leaders, the advice of *Rules to Win By* can be empowering. But its message can also obscure anti-democratic tendencies to treat workers like mere means to an end rather than agents of their own struggle. We need a sequel to McAlevey and Lawlor's important book that addresses these issues. Fortunately, its case studies are already being written by workers across the country.

UNMAKING ASIAN EXCEPTIONALISM
Gaiutra Bahadur

AS I WATCHED Pat Buchanan address the Republican National Convention three decades ago, I cried. I can still see his doughy face and fixed expression fill the TV screen as he urged his almost all-white audience: "We must take back our cities and take back our culture and take back our country." Buchanan's hardline anti-immigrant bid for the Republican nomination had been unsuccessful, but he was still waging his campaign to reclaim America's Judeo-Christian identity. At the time, I believed that he aimed his "we" and his "our" against me and my family. I felt it viscerally; in that long limbo after immigrating, my body was in a perpetually queasy state. I was seventeen, too young to vote but already made and unmade by the politics of race—by the coded language of candidates as well as by the racism that it enabled, racism as overtly menacing as the graffiti that once defaced our house. "Hindus Go Home," it directed.

In the late 1980s, in and around our neighborhood in Jersey City, New Jersey, our anonymous terrorizers and others who shared their hate at first used words as weapons. Then they deployed baseball bats, bricks, metal pipes, acid, their fists, their spit. A handwritten letter sent to the local newspaper published in August 1987 stated the goal: "We will go to any extreme to get Indians to move out of Jersey City." The manifesto's author revealed that his gang, in search of targets, scanned the phone book for Indian last names. They called themselves the Dotbusters—the name, like the slur "dothead," a riff on the red dot customarily worn on the forehead by some observant Hindu women. The writer bragged that there would be three "Patel attacks" later that night. A few days later, several blocks from us, a man with the last name Patel was beaten with a metal pipe while he slept in his home. After the newspaper published the Dotbusters letter, the attacks escalated: while walking down the street, a medical resident was beaten with a baseball bat, and a Citicorp employee out for drinks with a friend was pummeled with bricks. The first man emerged from his coma; the second didn't.

The incidents were among the most tragic in a years-long campaign of everyday intimidation that victimized South Asians of varying religions and nationalities but collapsed all into a "weak race"—to quote the Dotbusters manifesto—of "Hindus," used interchangeably with "Indians." The graffiti got my family partly right. We are Hindu but home was Guyana, on the northeastern coast of South America. Our ancestors left India four to five generations ago, as indentured workers contractually bound to labor in sugarcane fields, in a system denounced as a "new form of slavery" by British abolitionists. This history drew us close to Black Americans, opening possibilities for kinship even before we came to the United States. Like them, we are grandchildren of toil on plantations and grandchildren, too, of transoceanic traffic in the cargo holds of ships servicing empire and industry. This wrinkle in identity was lost on the bigots. Had they known, would it even have mattered? They encircled us. We were spat at on the street. Once, my father had to run from white teenagers who pulled knives on him outside the corner shop—but all things considered, we had been lucky. We escaped unhurt, physically.

In the late summer of 1992, when Buchanan spoke, we had been in the United States for a decade. My parents, new citizens, had done the remarkable. That year, through some uncanny frugality, my mother's frequent overtime as a clerk in New York's garment district, and my father's two jobs as a medical technologist at separate hospitals, they had paid off the mortgage on our house. It was a small red clapboard box that sat on the Palisades above the Hudson River, eyeing Manhattan. The house was humble and a little crowded—but it was ours, the first we had ever owned, in any country.

This was a matter of some pride for my parents because we had arrived in the United States with very little money. The regime we had fled allowed emigrants to leave with only the equivalent of $30 per person—and we were four. Nor did we have intergenerational wealth. What we did have was a support network in a large extended family. An aunt who came before us took us into her one-bedroom apartment when we landed, just as we took in relatives who came after us. My childhood taught me that family is figurative wealth. Only later did I realize that kin—who could provide first shelter, sponsor for green cards, and even cosign mortgages—could also, more concretely, be capital. I came to understand this as our privilege.

Growing up, however, I did not imagine us privileged. Instead, my psyche had been shaped by an acute sense that dispossession was our inheritance. We came from a community that had been twice displaced. Our right to belong had been challenged more than once, first by a racist dictatorship in Guyana, then by the Dotbusters in the Jersey City Heights. To buy a house, in the United States no less, was to assert belonging, somewhere special, somewhere safe. Descended from the history we were, becoming homeowners had symbolic, almost existential, weight. But the house was also a material claim to America, and I believe that vandals may have covered it in xenophobic graffiti—and thrown eggs, garbage, bricks, and firebombs at other South Asian homes and businesses in the city—because owning property triggered insecurities about being surpassed. We had left behind the 70 percent of our neighbors who rented, a statistic that eluded me at the time.

My parents had bought the house from a Polish American widow, the most recent in a long line of second- and third-generation Americans who had lived there in the century since it was built. All had been skilled contributors, according to census data, to the city's recently vanished industrial and manufacturing heyday: an electrician, a railroad clerk, longshoremen, a tool maker in a boiler works, a watchmaker. Mainly Catholic, like Buchanan, their parents and grandparents had migrated from Ireland, Italy, and Eastern Europe. By the 1980s, when we followed in their footsteps to this city behind the Statue of Liberty's back, historically a blue-collar immigrant gateway, it may have seemed like the pace of the American Dream had accelerated. We may have appeared to be living it, in the first generation.

A few weeks after Buchanan's convention speech, I went off to my freshman year at Yale, and this too was a piece of that accelerated Dream. That fall in New Haven, the Clintons visited campus on the campaign trail, and I felt an imposter's awe that the couple's alma mater might one day also, somehow, be mine. I was the first in my mother's line to attend college. On my father's side, he was the first and only one to get higher education. The Guyanese government had paid for college in exchange for his service in a volunteer para-military unit, and afterwards, he went to work for the country in the field laboratory of a nationalized sugar estate. In the United States, his foreign degree in the natural sciences did not pass muster with potential employers, and he had to earn a second bachelor's degree while working full time as an assistant warehouse manager. He had made his first Yankee dollars as a day laborer with a masonry crew run by an uncle. My father's own parents had been manual laborers, cutting cane and weeding, on the sugar plantation that had dictated our lives for generations. At the time, it must have unnerved him to think that immigrating might obliterate his hard-earned progress. It's clear, in retrospect, that we were on an upwardly mobile trajec-tory. I now teach journalism and literature as a professor on the very campus, Rutgers–Newark, that gave my father his second chance and gave our family our socioeconomic momentum. The summer I left for college, however, despite the house, despite the imminence of the Ivy League, our own class position still felt refutable.

At Yale I was misfit and often unsettled by my uphill bid to belong in a place whiter, richer, and more entitled than any I'd ever known. So overwhelmed was I that I didn't pay close attention to

Bahadur

two significant events that also made 1992 a consequential year in my cosmos. One concerned my hometown; the other, my home country. Both revealed the "war" for "the soul of America" that Buchanan said we were fighting: a struggle, in his words, for "who we are . . . what we believe and what we stand for as Americans."

THAT SEPTEMBER thirty years ago, federal prosecutors in New Jersey took three men, all white, to trial on hate crime charges for attacking the medical resident. Testimony placed the alleged perpetrators, our close neighbors, in a delinquent social world of drug users and dropouts who might easily have resented upstart rivals to the American Dream. The Heights, our shared neighborhood, was a white ethnic stronghold of lower-middle-class respectability but its underbelly was shot through with contradiction. The young men in the Dotbusters' orbit seemed frequently in trouble with the law, but some were also close to it. One of the defendants was a county police officer, and the other was the son of a high-ranking police official once in line to become the city's police chief. Despite eyewitness testimony and a confession, an all-white jury acquitted the men, thirty years ago this May. The case nonetheless made history as the first federal civil rights suit brought on behalf of a South Asian person in the United States.

For me the suit represents what we owe African Americans: the hope of equal protection under the law and a concrete tool for it. It goes without saying that we also owe them our very existence in America, since it was their movement for civil rights that laid the political groundwork for the 1965 immigration law that removed restrictions against people of Asian origin entering the United States. The Black struggle for justice also led to passage of the first federal hate crimes legislation in 1968. Crucially, these laws created the mechanism for federal prosecutors to step in when local law enforcement minimized the wide-scale attacks against South Asians, dismissed bias as a motive, and failed to pursue relevant leads. From the bench, the federal judge reprimanded local investigators for their inaction, saying he was "very disappointed" and comparing their failures to Nazi Germany's sanction of pogroms against Jews. With support from national Asian American organizations, South Asians in Jersey City had persisted in pushing for justice, taking to the streets to demand change, engaging in a tradition of nonviolent protest inspired by Martin Luther King, Jr., who in turn had been inspired by Mahatma Gandhi.

This postscript to the Dotbusters attacks sets an example for how African American and Asian American civil rights movements can gain ideas, energy, and spiritual momentum from each other. The full lesson, however, is more sobering and complicated.

By the 1980s Jersey City's foreign born made up a third of its population, and most of its newcomers were from Asia, Africa, the Caribbean, and Latin America. Its racial and ethnic makeup had been transformed in just a decade or two. There's evidence, such as handwritten membership cards found on some high school students and the manifesto published in the newspaper, that the Dotbusters—minimized by local officials as amorphous, more a rumor based on a set of uncoordinated attacks than an organized group—might have been a somewhat formalized underground association. Reacting to rapid demographic change, this gang of young white men foreshadowed the white supremacist groups now openly proclaiming themselves in our society, fulfilling my fear that our American Dream was revocable. But a few of the attacks against South Asians appeared to be copycat, unaffiliated, and carried out by other people of color. According to a 1987 *News India-Times* article, African American teenagers using anti-Indian slurs sprayed acid at the owner of a South Asian grocery store, burning him and his two-year-old daughter. The teenagers who were sentenced to a youth rehab center on assault charges for killing the Citicorp employee, as they reportedly, and mistakenly, taunted "Hindu, Hindu," (the victim was in fact Parsi, not Hindu) are Latino.

Those attacks point to an unnerving truth that has served the politics of divide and rule across centuries and borders. White supremacy can be so deeply embedded in the skin of societies that white skin itself is no prerequisite. People of color have committed violence against each other. Brown and Black solidarities are far from given. In the case of hate crimes against Asian Americans, an analysis of nationwide statistics from 1992 to 2014 shows that 26 percent were committed by other people of color, compared to 19 percent for Latinos and 1 percent for African Americans.

The use of the epithet "Hindu" by the Dotbusters and their copycats suggests one possible motive for violence that crossed ethnic lines: South Asians may have brought strange gods into their midst, in a context with an overwhelming Christian majority. At the height of the attacks, about a tenth of Jersey City's population had roots in Asia. Filipinos, predominantly Catholic, made up the largest subgroup, at 45 percent, and South Asians accounted for the second largest, at 28.5 percent. It's possible that, whether Hindu or Muslim or Parsi or Jain, we became the target at least partly due to our conspicuous religious difference.

The will to maintain power, if it's perceived to be under threat, and the pressure to protest the lack of it can both drive acts of hate. Both the presence and the absence of power can provoke violence, but power comes in many forms, operating at levels from the state to the street and intersecting in incongruous ways. In Jersey City in the late 1980s and early 1990s, the context was blue collar as well as Christian, and the configurations of power by virtue of religion, nativity, citizenship, racialization, and class were complicated and sometimes paradoxical.

The 1990 census depicts a city in pain, its unemployment and poverty rates high and its rates of educational attainment strikingly low. 8 in 10 Jersey City residents lacked a college degree; 34 percent didn't even have a high school degree. A disadvantaged class identity, like the dominant religious one, cut across several ethnic lines. Strictly by the numbers, Asian people in the city appeared to be faring better economically than African American, Latino, and white people, as classified by the U.S. Census Bureau. But the disparities were greater for other people of color: 12 percent of Asian residents lived in poverty compared to 15 percent of white residents, 25 percent of Black residents, and 27 percent of Latino residents, while 6 percent of Asian people were unemployed compared to 9 percent of white people, 15 percent of Black people, and 14 percent of Latino people. My family arrived in a city where the prospect of owning a home was tauntingly remote for most and clearly out of sync with the national picture. In 1970, a decade before we landed, only 31 percent of white residents in the city owned their own homes, and only 21 percent of Black residents did. Both groups owned homes at less than half the national rate of 65 percent. (The census gave no figures for home ownership among Latino or Asian residents that year.) Is it any wonder that the Dotbusters targeted property as well as people, or that some other people of color, struggling disproportionately, also participated?

"ASIAN," LIKE OTHER census-given identities, is too broad a category. It collapses into one a wide diversity of individual migration histories, as if the path of a Filipino recruited as a nurse on a work visa matches the path of a Vietnamese who landed as a refugee. The state and the street both do this reductive work. Society, through the model minority myth, in a sense flattens the identity Asian into a class. And yet the category also includes my very large West Indian immigrant family. Among the many dozens of us who resettled in Jersey City were nurses, construction workers, security guards, garment factory workers, delivery men, part-time college students, nannies, and office clerks. Still, we were probably targeted, at least in part, because we were grouped with a community perceived to have economic power and aspirational reach, through education.

When the attacks were at their height, I was in junior high, in a magnet program drawing the highest achievers from gifted and talented programs in public schools across the entire city, spanning its white neighborhoods, its Black ones, and all the ones in between. That was where I found my sense of belonging—not in owning a house, but with this band of twenty-eight super-nerd misfits, almost all immigrants or the children of immigrants. Although the city was then roughly a third white, only two of my classmates were. Two were Latino. And three were African American. That's how a census taker would have clocked us, but I didn't measure identity the way the census did. For me our bond as outsiders connected us, whether our parents had come from Colombia or China, India or Vietnam, Korea or the Ukraine, Pakistan or the Philippines (all points of origin for my classmates).

Looking at a photograph of our graduating class now, I register what I didn't then: we were overwhelmingly Asian, and fully a third of us had roots, recent or century-old, in South Asia. What seemed then like a meritocracy of strivers pixelates now into something far less clear: a disproportion that reflected structural inequalities in U.S. society, an exceptionalism that was probably at least partly produced by stereotyped expectations of a model minority, and one that no doubt further reinforced the stereotype, activating the Dotbusters and other perpetrators of hate crime.

The story of our coming to America begins in 1965. That year the Hart-Cellar Act ended half a century of racist exclusion in immigration law, overturning quotas and restrictions intended to keep the United States white, including bans on people of Asian origin. While lawmakers in D.C. were aligning immigration policy with the antiracist gains of the African American civil rights movement, with a law that would radically diversify the United States in the decades to come, an aunt in Guyana chanced on her own momentous and transformative opportunity. Reading the pulp crime magazine *True Detective*, a racy bit of Americana that she and her girlfriends regularly devoured, circulating each well-thumbed copy among themselves, she saw an ad from the Jersey City Medical Center. The hospital was looking for nurse trainees, and my aunt, at the time a midwife on a sugar plantation near our village, tore out the ad, defacing the communal copy. A year later, when Guyana became a free country, she left her husband and children behind to take the position she had succeeded in securing at the hospital. She landed in a city that was more than 85 percent white, where she lived with other foreign nurse trainees (mainly from the Philippines, South India, and the West Indies) in a dormitory in the hospital's complex of Depression-era, art deco stone high rises.

My aunt, the avid reader of *True Detective*, was the matriarch of our migration. The first to come, she forged the path for many dozens of Bahadurs to resettle in Jersey City. By the time my parents, my baby sister and I arrived in 1981, about half of the city's white population had fled, and the Asian population had more than tripled. The Black and Latino (mostly Puerto Rican) populations, which were numerically much larger, had grown, too, but not at such a dramatic rate. By the time the Dotbusters emerged, the Hart-Cellar Act had contributed to swift demographic changes that made my hometown a majority-minority city.

The influx of skill was another legacy of the Hart-Cellar Act. In addition to allowing Asians into the country in significant numbers for the first time, it shaped U.S. immigration policy in two other profound ways. First, it prioritized immigrants coming for higher education and high-skilled and professional work, giving birth to the stereotype of the successful Asian immigrant by admitting those already prepped and primed to achieve. And second, it also made family reunification a core principle, so much so that it was informally known as the "Brothers and Sisters" Act. It allowed the first wave to sponsor family members, who were not always as well set up for economic success, complicating the stereotype through richly diverse class identities and American experiences and highlighting just how much of a myth it is.

Like anti-Blackness, the model minority myth is easily exploited when power, at the level of the state, is at stake. In the history of the United States, both racializing ideas have sparked hostility and violence at the street level. The rhetoric of politicians who seek to divide has lit the fire. I wept at Buchanan's speech all those years ago because I felt targeted as a recent immigrant raised in the eye of anti-Indian violence. Listening to the speech again after decades, I realize that while Buchanan mobilized both anti-Blackness and anti-immigrant sentiment, it was mostly directed at African Americans. This forces me to see the story of my skin in a new light: our color had given us privilege even as it made us targets for the Dotbusters. Was it possible that I too had been seduced by the myth, tying up my identity with striving to do well, to prove my worth against the odds when the odds were already in some ways in our favor? The epiphany messes with my sense of self, but it expands it as well as destabilizes it.

At the close of his speech, Buchanan referred to the "riots" in Los Angeles, which had engulfed Korean-owned stores earlier that year, after a jury acquitted the police officers who had brutally beaten an African American man. Cameras panned to a pair of Asian American delegates in the convention hall as Buchanan called for "force rooted in justice," putting to work racialized stereotypes of the rules-abiding model immigrant versus the lawbreaking "mob." In an already charged context, his rhetoric further pit people of color against each other.

A SIMILAR STRATEGY worked in our home country as well. My family came to the United States pursuing economic mobility, but we were also fleeing racism rooted in imperial tactics of divide and rule. The dictatorship that we escaped had been installed by the United States as it maneuvered a Marxist out of power during the Cold War. It did so by manipulating tensions between Blacks and Indians first created by the policies of British colonial rulers in the previous century.

At slavery's end, instead of employing emancipated Africans at fair wages on the plantations, the British imported workers from India and China on exploitative contracts, paid them cheaply, and controlled them through a system that prosecuted two in five of them and convicted one in five of them, sending them to prison for labor violations. The discord thus began with indenture itself—a kind of global deployment of scab labor—and intensified as the British put African Guyanese in positions of power over the new workforce: they were, for instance, the "drivers" or sub-overseers, in charge of crews of Indian field laborers and the police constables who, sometimes fatally, suppressed plantation strikes and uprisings by Indian workers. By redirecting the resentments of the colonized to each other, rather than to their British masters, the state sought to stifle any united resistance to their rule.

The central struggle of my native country's life as an independent nation has been to break free from the legacies of this strategy of sowing conflict. As it was developing its own politics in the 1950s and 1960s, the U.S. government intervened, with the cooperation of the British, in ways that created two political parties not differentiated by policy, but by race. At its birth in 1966, Guyana became the first Black-led nation in the Western hemisphere without a Black majority. The leader ousted was Indian, and the leader installed, Black. Elections there had been rigged until October 1992—my freshman year in college—when former president Jimmy Carter, through his work at the Carter Center, was invited to oversee the first free and fair elections in the country in three decades. He helped to uphold democracy after John F. Kennedy's administration had dashed it.

IN THE TENSION between the idea and the reality of "who we are" and "what we stand for" as Americans, I do my work as a writer. I consider myself a lucky embodiment of the American Dream—lucky that my body was not broken with bricks or baseball bats for living it and lucky to have a body that, in a society beset by anti-Blackness, did not hinder my chances at it. Ever since the Dotbusters showed me how words could be weapons, I try my best to use America's uneven, ironic blessings to illuminate how we have been led to hate each other and how we might transcend that history.

Buchanan ran on an anti-Black and anti-immigrant platform because demagogues like him know only too well how profound—as Guyanese historian Walter Rodney put it—"people's power" can be. But if it can give white supremacy power, it can also rival it. We can resist how the state categorizes us. And the street can mean what we fight for it to mean. Solidarity, rather than a conflagration where people of color allow themselves to be manipulated against each other. The shape that populism takes is ours to mold.

My own contribution is to work toward an expanded sense of self: an "I" that redefines exceptionalism, my own and America's, by rejecting the concept entirely. I do this because, to echo Langston Hughes, "I, too, am America."

THE INTIMATE PROJECT OF SOLIDARITY

nia t. evans interviews Dan Berger, Gwendolyn Zoharah Simmons, & Michael Simmons

"FREEDOM IS A LOVE STORY," writes Dan Berger in the introduction of his recent book, *Stayed on Freedom: The Long History of Black Power through One Family's Journey.* "It is cacophonous and seamless, beautiful and tedious." Few authors illustrate that quite like Berger, who tells the little-known stories of Michael and Zoharah Simmons, activists whose decades of patient, dedicated organizing work—both locally and internationally—would help give lasting shape to the Black Power movement.

Berger follows Michael and Zoharah from their early married days in the Student Nonviolent Coordinating Committee (SNCC) to their separate, later efforts to dismantle apartheid in the 1980s and '90s. We watch as they and their comrades grow dissatisfied with the distance between SNCC's national leadership and the mid-1960s grassroots and decide to draft "The Black Consciousness Paper," an essay whose ideas will form the basis of what will eventually be known as Black Power politics. Michael and Zoharah traverse the globe, seeking various political homes—SNCC, the Quaker American Friends

Service Committee, the internationalist Third World Coalition—in which to nurture radical Black thought and power.

Stayed on Freedom is at times a complex portrait of a family and at others a history of a political movement. Indeed, it is often both at once, as each of the two makes significant personal sacrifices in service of their political mission. One memorable chapter details the then-couple's life in 1969. Zoharah gives birth to their first child, Aisha and, months later, Michael is arrested and imprisoned for his role in a Vietnam War draft protest. The Black freedom struggle, Berger's work reminds us, is precisely that: a challenging, risky, often dangerous process in which failure—failure to achieve a given material end, perhaps, or the breaking up of an organization over internal strategic disputes—sometimes occurs.

Yet Zoharah and Michael's Black Power politics refused to turn away from the messy, everyday work of organizing: the common view of Black Power as a retreat from political changemaking, the book emphatically reminds us, is a flawed one. Instead, the radical promise of the movement comes in what Berger calls its "intimate project of solidarity": an unashamed centering of Black pride while never forgetting the need to reach outward and build broad coalitions united around shared goals.

In May, nia t. evans sat down with Michael and Zoharah, along with Berger, to discuss the book and the two activists' ongoing work.

NIA T. EVANS: I want to start at the beginning. Michael and Zoharah, you both came to this work, in part, through the SNCC. How were you both introduced to the process of building political solidarity? What were your earliest lessons?

MICHAEL SIMMONS: Like most of my generational peers, I was ignorant about what to do. I was mad about what was going on, but I really didn't have things to educate me. My best notion of social change was through protests and demonstrations. But I never really thought about how you actually get people to protest. Growing up, there were only forays into what I consider the margins of the movement. In high school, I protested the treatment of Black workers with the Philadelphia NAACP, led by Cecil B. Moore. A couple years later, I, along with some other students at Temple University, organized a protest in solidarity with what was happening in Selma. But it wasn't until I worked with SNCC and began to see the nitty-gritty, day-to-day work of organizing and talking to people that I understood the antecedents to the protests I had been watching. SNCC helped me understand the relationship that is necessary between organizers and the people they claim to be fighting with.

ZOHARAH SIMMONS: I grew up living under Jim Crow apartheid in Memphis, Tennessee, and thinking back on it, I experienced Black people forming solidarity in organizations. By that, I mean churches, the Masonic and Eastern Star groups, the Knights of Labor. These were a part of my childhood. I didn't even think of them as spaces of solidarity until this very moment, but of course Black people had to band together and form these kinds of organizations to survive.

evans, Berger, Simmons, & Simmons

We grew up in situations where your life could be on the line at any point, so you had to build solidarity across race and class lines. I think about my second-grade teacher who was one of the first Black people to run for elected office in Memphis. Memphis was not like Mississippi: Black people could register to vote, but they rarely ran for office. So when she ran for office, the community came together to support her. They guarded her house, armed, twenty-four seven, because people threatened her life. She didn't win, but they kept her alive.

NTE: Dan, you've studied Black liberation movements for decades. What have you learned about the nature of political solidarity?

DAN BERGER: To me, solidarity is the benchmark or the standard of left politics. Back in 2005 I wrote a book about the Weather Underground that was born out of the global justice movement of the early 2000s, when there was such a passion for the idea of allies and allyship. That's part of what led me to want to write a book about the history of white antiracism. I came out of that book hating the framework of allyship. Allyship, as it was discussed in the early 2000s, presumed support for someone else's struggle. But I was most impressed with the extent to which the Weather Underground tried, albeit unevenly, to make anti-imperialism its own fight. And that's how I came to understand solidarity: that we have shared stakes in struggle. To be an "ally" in someone else's struggle is to suggest that our lives are unchanged by what happens in that struggle—that it doesn't matter if things change or stay the same. But I want to end patriarchy because it degrades my life and because I will be freer and better without it, as well as because it degrades the lives of women and nonbinary people. Solidarity is a much more meaningful and helpful rubric for understanding the work of social change.

We are engaged in a project of solidarity because we want the world to change. Michael put this perfectly at an event we recently did. He said, "I'm not an ally of anybody else. I am a participant in the struggle," and I think that sense of being coparticipants is key. Black power is an intimate project of solidarity, and that solidarity is not a rhetorical move, but something that needs to be expressed and practiced. Opening yourself up to struggling alongside others, placing your life in other people's hands as they have placed theirs in yours, is an incredible act of intimacy.

NTE: There's a fantastic discussion about solidarity in the book in relation to Michael's anti-apartheid work within the American Friends Service Committee (AFSC), a Quaker social justice organization that was amenable to his Black Power principles. Dan, you write that Michael hoped to make "solidarity more than pacifism the driving principle" for the group. Michael, can you talk about what that looked like in practice and Dan, how you came to describe it that way in your book?

MS: The AFSC was nonviolent in an absolute sense. Yet when we look at our lives, regardless of what our positions are, violence is everywhere. In the context of the freedom movement in Southern Africa, people tended to support the African National Congress

(ANC), which had explicitly turned away from its former policy of nonviolent resistance. But even though the American Friends Committee was, as far as I was concerned, ecumenical regarding the resistance forces in South Africa, the one thing that concerned everyone was the armed struggle, even though there were a range of tactics at play: the educational programs within the movement against apartheid in South Africa, the medical programs, the programs for women. I challenged my colleagues in the AFSC to look at all the range of nonviolent activity that was going on in the South Africa resistance and said that we needed to at least support those efforts.

But a lot of the conversations there were disingenuous. People found excuses for apartheid. The most notable was led by the Philadelphia minister (and General Motors board member) Leon Sullivan, who developed an alleged code of conduct for corporations doing business in South Africa that had no enforcement mechanism. There was virtually no monitoring of it. It amounted to a way for U.S. corporations to avoid being challenged on their financial support for apartheid. Against this dominant line, I convinced the AFSC to economically divest from South Africa and built a new project, Southern Africa Summer, to train a cohort of high school and college students in divestment organizing and anti-imperialist work.

I would say, within any given situation, regardless of what your political philosophy may be, 90 percent of the time, there's room for solidarity. We should not be looking for unanimous agreement on every single issue but trying to find the most salient ones and move from there.

DB: It makes me think of that Bernice Johnson Reagon idea that if you're in coalition, and you're comfortable, then you're not in coalition. There should always be some sort of generative tension if you are moving toward something. Michael's work in Southern Africa was so revelatory, in part, because it was about Southern Africa and not just South Africa. The mainstream narrative of the anti-apartheid movement was that it was focused on South Africa. But many adopted a regional approach, which engaged a much more expansive notion of solidarity and an anti-imperialist position.

A lot of people involved in those struggles were trying to name structural violence but didn't have the language. The very condition of apartheid was violent, and there was no way to be nonviolent in response. But I'm curious to hear Zoharah's perspective because the same issues that were happening in the AFSC and the broader 1970s peace movement in Southern African happened around Palestine twenty years later and are still happening in Palestine today. The convenience of asserting a sort of pacifist philosophy to avoid dealing with the primary violence of apartheid is one that has not gone away.

ZS: I first became involved in anti-occupation work because the AFSC had a vibrant Middle East program. And having been peripherally involved in the struggle against apartheid enabled me to see that those of us living in the United States could not tell people living under the boot of apartheid how best to respond to it. To be in solidarity meant doing whatever we could to make sure our government, which clearly had a big hand in keeping

evans, Berger, Simmons, & Simmons

the occupation going, changed its role and stopped supporting oppressive regimes.

DB: There's an AFSC article that came out in the early 1970s called "Nonviolence Not First for Export" by James Bristol. It calls to task this very dynamic we're describing: the idea that people in the West demand other struggles to be nonviolent as the precondition of their support. He argues that that's a misreading of nonviolence itself. That nonviolence has to begin from within. It's not first for export. And so, if you are a citizen of an imperial power, it's not for you to judge or demand a certain kind of tactical or philosophical allegiance from the people who are suffering under that empire.

NTE: Can we talk a bit about the coalitional politics behind the development of the Black Power movement? The Atlanta Project, the SNCC committee that publicly opposed the Vietnam War and developed Black Power principles, feels like a perfect example of the generative tensions we've been discussing. Michael and Zoharah, how did you come to be a part of the Atlanta Project?

ZS: At a young age, I understood that Black people were organizing to throw off the oppression they were living under. I grew up sitting in the back of the bus. It was Negroes on one side and whites on the other. And I had to give up my seat if they wanted it. The Atlanta Project simply named what we were always fighting for: Black power. We wanted it but we weren't usually saying it. Some people were. The Mississippi Freedom

Democratic Party, which built a new political process within an apartheid system, is a great example. That was about power. And it was mainly Black people.

During Mississippi Freedom Summer when SNCC, CORE and others joined forces to form the Council of Federated Organizations (COFO), I led the project to register voters in Laurel, MS. At least twenty of us were white, and there was always this situation where the Black people from Laurel thought that the white people were in charge. I was the project director, but if Black people came to the office and there was one white person there, they went to the white person to ask for help. And it really bothered me. We were all putting our lives on the line; the local community was, too. When we started the Atlanta Project after the Georgia legislature refused to let Julian Bond take his state congressional seat in 1966, we started talking about these things as a group. We recorded our experiences. The women in the group transcribed what we said, and then we'd read it and come back together again.

We realized we had some internal things we had to address that had been ingrained by years of slavery and Jim Crow and what we now call white supremacy. We had internalized it all. We saw ourselves as inferior. And in order to address it, we had to speak about it publicly to our white and Black comrades. One of the things we suggested was that whites needed to go into the white community to organize. That's where the seat of racism and white supremacy lies, and we, as Black people, couldn't change that without white comrades also being on board. But we also were clear that we had to address the issue of internalized racism. We had to get rid of it. We had to embrace the

evans, Berger, Simmons, & Simmons

notion of being Black, of being people of African descent, and loving ourselves in the skins we were in.

MS: I don't think that young Black people today really grasp how much we disrespected ourselves. Not just because of the lack of education or housing or jobs, but because of who we were. I can remember saying my prayers every night, and at the end of my prayer, I would say, "Dear God, please make my hair straight." And I did that for years. And I would put Vaseline in my hair. My brother and I would put stocking caps on it, and we'd look in the morning and see if there had been any progress. I had a friend whose mother used to pinch his nose in order to make it straight. People would try to bleach their skin. All these things kind of culminated within ourselves. I mean, nobody criticized Zoharah more than the African American community when she got an Afro in 1962. It was Black people who were freaked out by that. So Black power, from a cultural point of view, was a challenge to that. And suddenly, things changed. Almost overnight, we were wearing Afros and dashikis. We started thinking about Africa in a positive sense. All of that emanated, I would argue, from Black Power.

DB: The Atlanta Project is such a critical, overlooked, maligned story of how and where and who brought Black Power in and through the civil rights movement. The Project brought together all of the intimate scars of racism that Zoharah and Michael were just talking about in terms of self-hatred and self-disregard, but also a deep and abiding sense of internationalism.

It was a signature innovation within a long history of Black radicalism and internationalism. It brought to the moment in 1966 the reinvigorating sense that the war in Vietnam passed through Mississippi. That white supremacy was the apartheid South, but also this sense of self-hatred that was promulgated within Black communities. And it's a space where we can see both positive and failed examples of solidarity. When Michael and eleven other SNCC organizers were arrested after an antiwar demonstration, SNCC staff who were mad at the Atlanta Project for their articulation of Black Power still showed up at the jail and visited their comrades. There was a real strong sense of, "Well, we might be disagreeing politically, strategically, or really just personally, but we will still show up for you." And we see failed examples that culminated in Zoharah and Michael both being fired from SNCC after ongoing disputes between the national office and the Atlanta Project. There's a lot in the Atlanta Project that people have overlooked and misinterpreted, but it was a place where internationalism was developed in a practical, urgent way. And we see in these two people's lives how it has rippled across six decades of work grounded in international solidarity and exchange.

NTE: On that point, Zoharah, can you talk a bit about intergenerational organizing, international solidarity, and how the two might fuel each other?

ZS: My work at AFSC really helped to expand what had begun in SNCC. And SNCC had been involved in supporting the Palestinian struggle. Those of us on the AFSC staff got to engage with people from the Middle East, from Palestine, from Southern Africa. It was an amazing opportunity to grow and unpack the connections between U.S. imperialism and what was happening domestically and globally. It laid the groundwork for my life going forward. After that, I spent two years living in Jordan working with women attempting to change their lives for the better.

When I came to teach at the University of Florida, I focused on human rights. I always used to wonder when my students were going to get as fired up as we were, as I had become when I was their age. And then, of course, the murder of Trayvon Martin in 2012 lit a fire under young people here. I've been lucky enough to mentor and work with young people through the National Council of Elders and the SNCC Legacy Project. We're very focused on intergenerational dialogue. I just spent four days on Zoom with young people who were attending a National Council of Elders gathering. We discussed the issues of the day and what we elders have learned in our years of struggle. I see working with young organizers as critical to our forward momentum. We must internationalize our struggle and understand that we are battling imperialist forces within and beyond this country.

NTE: Where are you all seeing exciting sites of struggle and solidarity? What excites you? What concerns you?

MS: The Black Lives Matter movement excites me. Right now, people are protesting the death of Jordan Neely by laying on subway tracks. A multiracial, multigenerational group of people—that's a beautiful thing. We love to tell the stories of movements in short vignettes and often forget that they're long processes. And movements are messy. They're not a straight line. But people are trying new things, coming together.

But of course, what concerns me is Trumpism. These people cannot win democratically, so what they're slowly trying to do is take away our right to vote, which, when you think about the arc of the civil rights movement, is where we started. I'm really concerned about that trend. It needs to stop.

zs: I, too, was heartened to see people stopping the subway trains and to see the bravery of those people fighting for Jordan Neely. So that encourages me. What I want to see is some big-tent organizing that brings us together with some concrete goals. There are so many issues—everything from Cop City, the proposed police training facility in Atlanta that has sparked mass protests and resistance, to abortion rights, to housing inequality, to our health care system. In the civil rights era, we utilized coalitions. We had SNCC, the NAACP, and other groups form COFO. I want to see that kind of coalition building again. These are the questions I'm asking when I talk to my younger comrades. How do we have a big tent that fights the right-wing, neofascist forces we're up against?

db: I agree with my comrades here. There's a lot that concerns me about this moment. We're facing rising authoritarianism, nationalism, climate chaos, and a series of sort of patriarchal nightmares. And it's all connected. Honestly, solidarity is the only way out of any of this. The same people behind Cop City are the people pushing anti-trans legislation and essentially bribing Supreme Court justices. We're up against the same forces operating in all these different domains. But there are also all these moments of exciting pushback with people like Justin Jones and Justin Pearson, whose protests against their expulsions from the Tennessee House of Representatives led one article to label them the "New Faces of Black Power Politics." People are starting to recognize this is all a part of the same struggle: not only are we facing the same enemies, but we're broadly pursuing shared goals. I always come back to the slogan of "one no and many yeses." It's still a good orienting point for this moment.

zs: I love that. One no and many yeses.

ESCAPE FROM THE MARKET

Simon Torracinta

WHEN THE CARES ACT slated $1,200 "economic impact payments" for most American adults in the early throes of the pandemic, advocates of universal basic income (UBI) could be forgiven for imagining that their long-cherished ideal at last might become reality. The times seemed uniquely propitious: two more impact payments followed in 2020 and 2021, and the American Rescue Plan further increased cash transfers through significant expansions of unemployment benefits as well as child, dependent care, and earned income tax credits.

Dreams of a guaranteed income are longstanding, but they leapt back into the public imagination in the wake of the 2008 financial crash, endorsed by a diverse array of figures on both left and right. By 2020 presidential candidate Andrew Yang briefly managed to catapult himself into the media spotlight by pitching an eye-catching "Freedom Dividend" of $1,000 a month to every U.S. citizen over the age of eighteen. Building on this momentum, the nearly unprecedented use of fiscal firepower during the pandemic seemed poised to effect a permanent transformation of the welfare system in both the United States and across much of the Global North.

Yet as soon as U.S. economic growth began to revive and inflation began to tick upward, a chorus of economists and employers blamed the emergency relief measures for overheating the economy. Today inflation anxiety continues to dominate headlines, the impact payments have entirely stopped, and every pandemic-era expansion of the transfer system has been allowed to quietly expire. With the end of the expanded child tax credit, 3.7 million more children plunged below the poverty line, and food insufficiency for families with children has increased by 25 percent. Basic income seems as far from reality as it ever has been.

Given its frequent selling point as a "utopia for pragmatists"—one endorsed by Yanis Varoufakis, Charles Murray, and Mark Zuckerberg alike—why is basic income always on the cusp of implementation, a dream perpetually deferred? This is the question that Anton Jäger and Daniel Zamora Vargas never quite answer in their illuminating book, *Welfare for Markets*, a global history of arguments for basic income. Though Jäger and Zamora call their project a "social history of ideas," they largely focus on the writings of intellectuals and poli-cymakers. As they see it, the proliferation of basic income proposals in recent decades—even by some thinkers on the left—reflects our warped political imagination under the triumph of market ideology. UBI poses so little threat to market hegemony, they suggest, that it is a virtual fait accompli. (In other writings, the authors have explicitly rejected what they call UBI's "anti-normative instinct," which accepts "a highly individualist notion of 'needs,' in many ways compatible with the 'consumer sovereignty' trumpeted by neoliberals.")

The broader history lurking in the margins of the book suggests a different conclusion: that even modest forms of basic income keep being beaten back precisely because they threaten the work incentives on which our market order relies. Far from spelling the *end* of meaningful politics, basic income is one site where it can and has flourished—and where the structures underlying our economic life have often been laid bare.

JÄGER AND ZAMORA, both Belgian, are prolific historians of modern political thought with distinctly cosmopolitan interests, sensitive to the transnational traffic of ideas and the strangeness a country's politics can take on in comparative perspective. They showcase this wide-ranging approach in *Welfare for Markets*, which covers developments across the globe—in the United States, Britain, France, Belgium, the Netherlands, South Africa, India, Mexico, and beyond—while deftly weaving together English, French, and Dutch sources.

The book opens with what Jäger and Zamora call an "anti-mythology." Present-day basic income advocates, eager to project a noble lineage for the idea, invoke figures such as Englishmen Thomas More and Thomas Paine and French socialist Charles Fourier as illustrious predecessors. *Welfare for Markets* convincingly debunks this genealogy. Early modern thinkers were united in thinking that Roman agrarian laws, which sought to redistribute landed holdings, led to the ruin of the republic. As a result, they sought less radical means of achieving republican liberty. This anxiety lay behind More's recommendation, in

Utopia (1516), "to provide everyone with some means of livelihood"—a form of in-kind provision intended as an alternative to the Roman example. The same fear motivated Paine's proposal, in *Agrarian Justice Opposed to Agrarian Law* (1796), for a "National Fund" to be "paid to every person"—not as a radical act of leveling but "a compensation in part, for the loss of his or her natural inheritance, by the introduction of the system of landed property." Even Fourier's proposal for a "decent minimum" for living in his "Letter to the High Judge" (1803) was implicitly to be paid in kind, since his imagined utopia was to be free of money altogether.

The modern notion of a basic income—continuous, unconditional cash payments—is a far cry from these in-kind proposals. As historian Peter Sloman shows in *Transfer State* (2019), its roots lie in proposals for a "state bonus" or "social dividend" in the Fabian circles of interwar Britain, which were keen to use the transfer apparatus of the state to lessen social injustice while at the same time avoiding undermining incentives to work. Although Jäger and Zamora touch on this early history, for them the modern history of basic income really begins with the negative income tax (NIT), first formulated by none other than economist Milton Friedman in the early 1940s. Long before Friedman won notoriety as a popular free-market partisan, *Welfare for Markets* shows, he was a consummate technician of the New Deal, working in the National Resources Committee and the National Bureau of Economic Research before landing at the U.S. Treasury.

At the time, prevailing wisdom endorsed state-organized re-structuring of markets and often the direct provisioning of goods like housing, employment, or health care. Yet rather than tackling poverty and inadequate employment through the post–New Deal bureaucracy, Friedman asked, why not simply enact "negative" rates within the federal income tax system, ensuring a minimal floor of income for all individuals below a given threshold?

As a matter of feasible public policy, this proposal would have been unthinkable only a few years prior. The fiscal firepower needed to fight World War II had only recently driven a massive expansion of the federal income tax, which came to cover a majority of the population for the first time in U.S. history. In this climate, Friedman's work in the bowels of the administrative state in the late 1930s proved instrumental in inspiring the idea of an NIT. To help calculate the "standard of living" estimates so central to New Deal policy, Friedman had been tasked with constructing consumption indices from nationwide survey data. The task involved ultimately arbitrary determinations of which goods counted as necessary purchases. A far simpler solution, Friedman came to believe, was simply to use cash transfers to set a minimum standard that individuals could spend as they saw fit.

Put so simply, the idea has a certain intuitive appeal. Yet it also rode the coattails of key intellectual developments. The economics profession of the interwar period had been deeply shaped by the "socialist calculation debate" over the possibility of a directly planned economy. Many economists began to stress the unique capabilities of a free market price system, and the field became increasingly hostile to collective or state-led determination of needs. Instead, welfare came to be measured by the aggregate satisfaction of individual preferences, and many economists maintained that because individual desires were incommensurable, economics had no scientific basis on which to advocate income redistribution. By the late 1930s these propositions had become the foundation of Anglo-American "neoclassical" economics, so much so that even left-leaning economists in this period began to endorse the price system.

Within this paradigm, the NIT had the advantage that it could ameliorate the worst excesses of market society—ensuring a basic income floor—without interfering with individual consumer choice or the efficient allocation of the market as a whole. Quite unlike the New Deal or the welfare state, it left the price system untouched. Crucially and radically, too, unlike conventional forms of social security or earlier transfer proposals, the NIT was designed as an "antipaternalist" measure that fully delinked transfers from work or other behavioral requirements.

AS LATE AS the 1950s, the NIT and similar grant proposals had not circulated far beyond narrow circles of economists and policymakers. There were good reasons for this marginality, Jäger and Zamora suggest. The immediate postwar period was defined by the interlocking imperatives of high growth, full employment, and Keynesian stabilization. These "welfare worlds" of midcentury were underpinned by mass parties pushing for programs that met specific needs—like social housing—both within work and outside it, and the NIT's presuppositions were entirely out of step with such developments.

The terrain began to shift in the early 1960s with the dramatic "rediscovery" of poverty in the United States as epitomized by tracts like Michael Harrington's *The Other America* (1962). In this context, Friedman's NIT proposal, republished in his bestseller *Capitalism and Freedom* of the same year, suddenly received a wider and more positive reception. Over the course of the 1960s, both the persistence of poverty—newly visible in sophisticated income statistics and increasing welfare rolls—and the new specter of "automation" as a threat to full employment contributed to basic income's growing and heterogeneous appeal.

For "commercial Keynesian" economists in Washington like James Tobin and Walter Heller (architect of the 1964 tax cut), fiscal policy was above all a technical question of fine-tuning aggregate demand. As they saw it, basic income had the advantage of elegance and simplicity, quite unlike the inefficient social programs whose social dimensions of solidarism or mutuality they largely disregarded. Meanwhile, a manifesto on "The Triple Revolution" in 1964—signed by signatories as diverse as chemist Linus Pauling, futurologist Robert Theobald, economist-sociologist Gunnar Myrdal, and Students for a Democracy Society leaders Todd Gitlin and Tom Hayden—warned of the possible "disappearance of work" in the age of cybernetics and directly endorsed an "unqualified right to an income" inspired by the NIT. Momentum ramped up, particularly within academic and policy circles. By 1968 more than a thousand economists had signed on to the idea in an open letter, with prominent economist Paul Samuelson boasting in *Newsweek* that "any plan that simultaneously commands the allegiance of professor Milton Friedman and John Kenneth Galbraith must have a lot going for it."

The vision of an imminent future beyond work found its most radical expression in the work of Detroit autoworker James Boggs, who had already witnessed the early waves of automation-driven job loss in his own plant through the 1950s, the canary in the coalmine for the dramatic onset of deindustrialization that would engulf the urban Black workforce first and hardest. "How can the labor movement speak for Negroes," Boggs declared in 1962, "when . . . 76 percent of Negro youth in Detroit are unemployed?" As he argued in *The American Revolution* (1963), the inexorable forces of automation required a radical remaking of socialism, built on the principle that "everyone has a right to full life, liberty, and the pursuit of happiness, whether he is working or not."

Boggs had signed the Triple Revolution manifesto in 1964, and similar fears about the disappearance of work would lead Martin Luther King to endorse basic income by 1967 in the wake of his Poor People's Campaign—a notable contrast to the job guarantee and expansive Keynesian vision of the "Freedom Budget" drafted by labor-aligned leaders of the civil rights movement only a year earlier. Meanwhile, 1966 saw the establishment of the National Welfare Rights Organization (NWRO), an organization of welfare recipients—nearly all women with children—who argued for fully removing work requirements and discriminatory "man-in-the house" rules from the welfare system. When sociologists Richard Cloward and Frances Fox Piven infamously proposed overwhelming the welfare system through mass enrollment in 1966, they declared that their "ultimate objective" was "to wipe out poverty by establishing a guaranteed annual income."

By 1969 the idea of a guaranteed income had gathered enough steam that Daniel Patrick Moynihan won over President Richard Nixon in support for a proposed bill, the Family Assistance Plan (FAP), that would have ensured up $1,600 a year (roughly $12,500 today) for all families under a given income threshold. For Moynihan, who had authored a notorious 1965 report identifying family dysfunction as the root cause of Black poverty, the FAP presented a single sweeping solution to the built-in "disincentives to family formation" *and* the extensive social service bureaucracy of the existing welfare system. Opposed by advocates on the left (like the NWRO) for being too meager and by those on right (like the U.S. Chamber of Commerce) for reducing incentives to work, the FAP passed the House in 1970 but ultimately failed in the Senate. The compromises that emerged in its wake—Supplemental Security Income and the Earned Income Tax Credit—certainly transformed the U.S. fiscal landscape, institutionalizing means-tested and conditional forms of cash transfers and tax subsidies. But by the early 1970s, the wave of interest in basic income dissipated as rapidly as it had crested. A proposed annual "demogrant" of $1,000 per person was not enough to save the 1972 George McGovern campaign from an ignominious defeat. A genuine basic income appeared dead in the United States.

Yet the story of basic income in Europe had only just begun. Throughout the late 1970s and early 1980s, Jäger and Zamora chronicle, a diverse cast of leftist thinkers increasingly sought to break with what they took to be the backward-looking "producerism" and cumbersome administrative state they associated with mainstream social democratic parties and trade unions. Many French advocates of *autogestion* (workers' self-management) became convinced that automation and computing held out the promise of an imminent "cybernated" economy characterized by abundant free time. Meanwhile the libertarian currents of the post-1968 left nursed growing skepticism of what sociologist Pierre Bourdieu called the "exercise in stigmatization" and the "politics of disciplinarization and normalization" around the existing social security system.

Work itself increasingly came under scrutiny, as in the Austrian-French theorist André Gorz's best-selling *Farewell to the Working Class* (1980), which proclaimed that "productive activity" had "been emptied of its meaning, its motivations, and its object," and that the present goal ought to be "to free oneself *from* work." To this emergent "postwork" left, an unconditional cash transfer free of work requirements—with which each individual could do precisely as they wished—offered a vision of individual autonomy and creativity beyond labor. Inspired in part by Gorz, the new Political Party of Radicals in the Netherlands proclaimed its support for a *basisinkomen* in 1982, and a year later the self-proclaimed "Dutch Council against the Work Ethic" held an "anti-May Day" protest in defiance of corporatist trade unions and the work ethic.

WELFARE FOR MARKETS does not explain the uneven geographical uptake of basic income in Europe, but the neighboring Dutch ferment did provide an inspiration to the notable Belgian philosopher Philippe Van Parijs, who first sketched out his blueprint for his "*impôt négatif*" in 1982.

Trained at Oxford in the "analytical Marxist" tradition, Van Parijs proposed a version of basic income that sought to develop a "capitalist road to communism" marrying socialist values of egalitarianism and the progressive abolition of labor to the policy tools and principles of neoclassical efficiency. His vision was decidedly iconoclastic: "Why not," Van Parijs and his coauthors in the Collectif Charles Fourier wrote in 1984, "get rid of employment insurance, legal pensions, state benefits and aid, study allowances . . . and state subsidies for ailing industries" and replace them entirely with a single stipend? In this vision, everyone would receive a sum sufficient to cover living expenses "regardless of whether the person in question was employed or unemployed, rich or poor, whether the person lived alone, with family, in partnership, or in a wider commune." But this wasn't all: for the Collectif, the basic income ought to be paired with deregulation of the labor market, the abolition of limits to the working day, of the minimum wage, the minimum age of schooling, and the maximum retirement age. "Do all of this," the authors wrote, "and simply observe what will happen."

The great advantage of proposals like UBI, Van Parijs maintained elsewhere, was precisely that "the beautiful simplicity of the left-right axis is pulverized before our eyes." Van Parijs's advocacy and organizational work would be critical in knitting together the diverse tendencies and thinkers that culminated in the Basic Income European Network (BIEN), which held its founding conference in Belgium in 1986. Rechristened as the Basic Income *Earth* Network in 2004, BIEN remains the main advocacy organization for UBI worldwide.

It is not a coincidence that an academic philosopher has proved so central to basic income's trajectory. While Jäger and Zamora do not press this point, the late 1980s are precisely the moment when basic income largely retreated back into technocratic and academic milieux. As in the United States, basic income ideas in Europe never fully crossed the threshold from speculative proposal to mass demand, let alone actual implementation. Cash transfers have become the social program of choice on both sides of the Atlantic, with subsidies or vouchers replacing all manner of direct public provision. Aside from a continual froth of UBI "experiments," a genuinely unconditional and universal income floor has never been introduced in sustained fashion anywhere.

Though the politics of basic income have consistently failed to cross the finish line in Europe and North America, *Welfare for Markets* documents a fascinating third act in the Global South. In the immediate postwar period, the main paradigm of economic development called for large, planned investments, rapid industrialization, and import substitution as means of catch-up growth and modernization. Even as this model faltered in 1970s, Third World countries organized to advocate a major restructuring of the world economy and the terms of international trade through proposals like the New International Economic Order. But with the debt crisis of the 1980s and the growing intransigence of rich countries, international development began to pivot to a significantly more constrained model of poverty alleviation.

Within this increasingly technocratic vision, "conditional cash transfers" (CCTs)—small and direct cash payments typically "conditional on recipients' specific behavior patterns, such as children's school attendance, visits to health clinics, or labor market participation"—became popular among both domestic elites and international development circles. The appeal was that such policies could palliate, without disrupting, a suite of market-oriented "structural adjustments" and liberalization measures targeting nationalized industries, public sector employment, in-kind benefits, and state subsidies across the Global South, often with devastating social effects. Pioneered by the African National Congress in postapartheid South Africa in the mid-1990s, the model soon spread across the world. There were 123 transfer programs in southern Africa by 2012 alone, and flagship programs like Progresa in Mexico and the Bolsa Família in Brazil attracted significant international attention.

In their zeal to paint any invocation of basic income in an "anti-normative" light, Jäger and Zamora attempt to link this CCT revolution to the advocacy of economists like BIEN cofounder Guy Standing, who has influentially argued for expanded and truly unconditional basic income as the only realistic program for economies apparently fated to permanently stagnant growth, high unemployment, persistent precarity, and sprawling informal sectors. Yet the gap between these two visions is huge: as in Europe and the United States, the policy consensus in the Global South has congealed around a set of far more targeted and limited transfers than the income floor imagined by utopians on both left and right. CCTs are neither universal or unconditional; in other words, they are nowhere close to a true UBI.

Jäger and Zamora are right, however, that as informal work and economic stagnation have spread to the Global North, the idea of basic income has gained some traction once again. Surveying what they call our post-2008 "technopopulist" moment, they note that UBI proposals have been embraced by Silicon Valley executives who again predict an automation catastrophe, by a new generation of "postwork" theorists on the left, and by heterogeneous populist formations—from the Five

Star Movement in Italy to Andrew Yang—that are drawn to UBI's scrambling of conventional left/right binaries. More conventional policy circles have expressed interest, too: since 2022 the City of Chicago has run the largest UBI experiment of its kind in the United States, offering an unconditional $500 a month to a lottery-selected sample of five thousand residents.

Rather than "monocausal neoliberalism," Jäger and Zamora argue, the "global rise of cash transfers" hints at "a deeper and messier market turn that ran through many traditions and currents in the late twentieth century." Quoting from French philosopher Marcel Gauchet's account of the "second capitalist revolution" of the latter half of the twentieth century, *Welfare for Markets* concludes that it is the consumer, rather than the worker or citizen, who stands as the central subject for a world in which money has "found its proper place . . . an orbit which rises and sets like some artificial sun."

AS AN EXPRESSION of political despair, the metaphor is clear enough. But can this metaphysic of money do the work Jäger and Zamora ask of it, given that social life has been mediated by money and markets in the Global North for several centuries now? As the authors remind us with the book's first epigraph, Karl Marx had already offered a trenchant critique of the "cash nexus" by the 1840s, nearly a century *before* the height of the solidaristic politics whose downfall the book justifiably laments. If the monetary mediation of life is really so corrosive, it is hard to see how the New Deal could emerge in a country where life insurance had been a mass industry since the Civil War. In her reading of Virginia Woolf's *A Room of One's Own* (1929), political theorist Alyssa Battistoni observes that money is first and foremost a means to life itself. When Woolf marveled at a small bequest that left her a fixed allowance for life, her elation was had nothing to do with promiscuous consumption. "It is remarkable," Woolf observed, "what a change of temper a fixed income will bring about. No force in the world can take from me my five hundred pounds. Food, house and clothing are mine forever."

One might expect to encounter this perspective in the words of transfer recipients themselves. Yet in perhaps the biggest shortcoming of the intellectual historical orientation of *Welfare for Markets*, such voices are entirely absent. Firmly ensconced in the world of planners, economists, utopians, technocrats, philosophers, and the occasional activist, the book overlooks the views of the poor, who are portrayed in precisely the same abstract fashion that Jäger and Zamora decry when it comes to economic theory.

In the exception that proves the rule, *Welfare for Markets* invokes the congressional testimony of NWRO Vice President Beulah Sanders only to liken her pleas for support to the notorious thesis of the Moynihan report. (In reality the NWRO's members produced a fascinating repertoire of arguments about the role of welfare support in the micropolitics of domestic life.) The absence of the poor in Jäger and Zamora's analysis is all the more surprising given the well-known historical tendency of social programs—and cash transfers, in particular—to generate entrenched constituencies, with significant political consequences. This fact, already acknowledged by Dwight Eisenhower in 1954—"should any political party attempt to abolish social security, unemployment insurance . . . you would not hear of that party again in our political history"—was also clearly recognized by the unlikely figures of Donald Trump and Jair Bolsonaro, both of whom sought to ramp up transfers ahead of their reelection campaigns.

It may be that Jäger and Zamora are tempted by a metaphysical conclusion—that the rise of basic income proposals is at once the inevitable expression and unwitting handmaiden of the advance of market logic—precisely because their focus on ideas tends to obscure the political, institutional, and social conditions in which they have always been embedded. It is only by zooming out from ideas and arguments about basic income that the broader picture comes into view. In contrast to the loose theorization of "technopopulism" in *Welfare for Markets*, for example, cultural theorist Michael Denning has recently proposed that we think of populism as the expression of the livelihood struggles that cluster around what Marx once called the "secondary" forms of exploitation in democratic polities. By this Marx meant the distinctively modern forms—taxes, rent, debt, mortgage, interest—through which the social surplus is divided and fought over outside of and beyond the wage.

From this perspective, struggles over taxes and transfers are often class politics in another key—not necessarily evidence of the hypnotism of the market. Jäger and Zamora appear to suggest that post-1960s visions of guaranteed income and struggles over welfare payments in the United States posed little challenge to the existing political-economic order, but this wasn't how many entrenched interests saw it. The Californian anti-tax revolts of the 1970s, powered by suburban homeowners angry over fiscal transfers, developed the mass base of the New Right and ultimately propelled Ronald Reagan into office. From this vantage, basic income—and transfer payments more generally—look not so much like the product of a singular "market turn" but instead like one front in a far broader terrain set out by the expansion of the fiscal state, the longstanding financial intermediation of daily life, and the changing patterns of work and family.

Indeed, the book's narrow focus on intellectuals also obscures the broader purchase that basic income had at any given time. We are told both that basic income ideas gained steam during the 1960s war on poverty but also that Johnson was implacably opposed. Jäger and Zamora devote significant attention to the social pressure campaigns of the postwork left, yet they also concede that Dutch Labor Party repeatedly affirmed its commitment to full employment even during the 1980s high water mark of agitation—a pattern broadly repeated across the European social democratic parties, with basic income falling entirely off the mainstream agenda through the 1990s. More recently, a straightforward referendum on a basic income proposal in Switzerland in 2016—whose GDP per capita exceeds that of the United States—saw a fairly staggering defeat, with 77 percent voting against. And despite the apparent rise of "technopopulism" in the 2010s, Yang's viral endorsement of the policy for his 2020 presidential campaign netted him a humiliating 2.8 percent of votes cast in the New Hampshire democratic primary. So much for the triumph of the sovereign consumer.

The apparent paradox of intellectual success and political margin- ality can be resolved only by taking a broader view. It has always been far cheaper for the state to police, control, and imprison the castoffs from market society than to engage in the genuine redistribution that even the most minimal floor of basic income would require. This goes a long way to explaining the highly limited and conditional nature of nearly all actually existing cash transfers worldwide. As Zamora has noted elsewhere, even a fairly modest proposal of €1,100 ($1,300) a month (in addition to existing benefits) in France was costed at 35 percent of GDP. A genuinely emancipatory UBI at a level high enough to avoid subsidizing existing forms of precarious and low-wage employment, moreover, has always had a still more serious count against it: undercutting the compulsion to work would severely undermine the power of the employer class.

This is why basic income is fundamentally inimical to capitalists—the same reason, as it happens, that economist Michał Kalecki famously identified regarding full employment. Although *Welfare for Markets* does not attempt such an account, one might even see the booms and busts of basic income thinking in the Global North as related to what Kalecki called the "political business cycle," with upswings of interest in periods of serious economic dislocation (in the late 1960s/early 1970s and after 2008) and decline in periods of tighter labor markets or greater stability (the 1950s, 1990s, and perhaps now the 2020s).

Jäger and Zamora are certainly right to decry the neoclassical outlook that refuses to consider any "inefficient" collective or in-kind provision of needs and benefits. At a minimum, any halfway adequate response to the threat of climate catastrophe will require a total break with worship of the sovereign consumer and the market deference built into the microeconomic tools that guide policymaking today. It will also require a critical theory of needs—one that understands how they are socially and collectively determined, rather than pure expressions of individual desire. Rapid decarbonization simply cannot rely on the aggregate outcome of individual consumer decisions, no matter how many or how sophisticated the "nudges" or "incentives." It will require dramatic public intervention to reshape the basic infrastructure of life itself, and ultimately, perhaps, even democratic control over the investment function.

Progressive advocates of basic income must bear the burden of explaining why it will not naturalize an individualist ethos that prevents collective action in the face of climate emergency. But it is essential to recognize that what stands in the way of their vision is precisely what stands in the way of the future Jäger and Zamora want. Loosening the yoke of market compulsion through any instrument—in cash or in kind, through transfer or through contract, via the workplace or the state—will require enough power to overcome the same entrenched interests. *Pace* John Maynard Keynes, who thought that "the power of vested interests" was "vastly exaggerated compared with the gradual encroachment of ideas," the world is ruled by little else.

Editors' Note: This essay is a condensed and lightly edited version of a review that first appeared online in May.

THE ABORTION PLOT

Judith Levine

NOT LONG AFTER the passage of Texas SB 8—the 2021 law that banned abortion at six weeks and allowed anyone to sue anyone who "aids or abets" the termination of a pregnancy—a Galveston County resident used the law against the women who helped his wife procure pills for a self-managed abortion. Two of the three women, Jackie Noyola and Amy Carpenter, filed a counterclaim against the man, Marcus Silva. In it they filled in the story of his longtime emotional and physical abuse of Brittni Silva, his attempts to prevent her from divorcing him, and his scheme to win a million-dollar bounty.

"Jackie's and Amy's only offense was their willingness to talk with Brittni about her options, share information about available resources, and ultimately support her decision to self-administer abortion medication so as to terminate a possible pregnancy," the countersuit reads. "In essence, they are being sued because they were good friends. Indeed, Jackie and Amy are the friends we all wish we had. They gave Brittni solace and safe harbor when Silva sought to abuse and control her. They helped her break the cycle of emotional abuse. They don't deserve to be sued; they deserve to be applauded."

What Jackie and Amy did for Brittni is beautiful, but it is ordinary—or it *was* ordinary between 1973 and 2022, after *Roe v. Wade* and before *Dobbs v. Jackson Women's Health Organization*, the Supreme Court case that overturned *Roe*. That ordinariness represents a huge achievement of the fight to decriminalize abortion—the defeat of shame and isolation. A movement was born when a secret went public and an individual problem became a shared one, when personal support became mutual aid and mutual aid coalesced into solidarity.

The right has worked indefatigably—and not without success—to revive the shame of abortion. In the year since *Dobbs*, antiabortion lawmakers are legislating the isolation. By devising forms of surveillance that turn acquaintances, colleagues, and even family members into potential informants, and by instituting penalties as severe as life imprisonment, the antis have made it perilous to be a friend.

This does not mean that no one will dare to help abortion seekers, now that it is banned or severely restricted, or expected to be soon, in nearly half of states. The aiders and abettors, like Jackie and Amy, may be moved by personal love, political conviction, or both. If bodily autonomy belongs to the individual, the concept of reproductive justice reminds us that pregnancy, childbirth, and childrearing (and their refusal) are not just bodily, not just political, but also social—socially determined and socially enacted. The story of abortion and its prohibition, in other words, is always a story of relationship.

This is the lesson of a long line of films about unwanted pregnancies. And whereas in the past the drama usually unfolded within the tense privacy of the heterosexual couple—or focused on the pregnant woman alone—contemporary abortion films overwhelmingly narrate the stories of women's friendship and solidarity. In doing so, they also explore how antiabortion laws can strain even the truest friendships and how feminist solidarity can keep reproductive liberty alive when individual acts of love become too risky.

THE DEVASTATING *4 Months, 3 Weeks and 2 Days* (2007), by writer and director Cristian Mungiu, transpires over one day in 1987 in an unnamed city in Romania. Abortion had been legal in Romania from 1957 to 1966; during that decade, with reliable contraception unavailable, 80 percent of pregnancies ended in abortion. No doubt for complex reasons, including the penury of life in communist Romania, the birth rate plummeted. Dictator Nicolae Ceaușescu blamed the decline on abortion and instituted far-reaching pronatalist policies, including mandatory gynecological exams of unmarried women, the prohibition of contraception, and the criminalization of almost all abortions, with heavy penalties both for patient and provider. Between 1965 and 1989, more than nine thousand women died from complications from illegal abortion.

In *4 Months*, Găbița (Laura Vasiliu), a university student, has an abortion, and her roommate Otilia (Anamaria Marinca) goes to extraordinary lengths to help her. Găbița is a flake, with an almost infantile demeanor. She flubs the hotel reservation, and sends Otilia to meet the abortionist in her stead, against his instructions (Why? "It was really hard for me," Găbița later explains). She cannot find the money; Otilia asks her boyfriend, Adi, without telling him why. Găbița brings homemade cakes to the abortion but forgets the specified plastic sheet. She lies about details small and large, including the stage of her pregnancy: over four months.

Each misstep increases the power of the abortionist, a menacing misogynist named Mr. Bebe. His every word insinuates and humiliates. "Why should somebody else pay for your actions? Was it me fooling around?" he asks. He explodes when Otilia tries to negotiate the now much higher fee. "Do you think I'd risk ten years for 3,000 lei? What do you take me for, an idiot?" But there are other chips to ante. "If I'm nice to you, won't you be nice to me?" he coos. He moves to walk out; Găbița begs him to stay. Otilia sits on the bed and takes off her clothes. Găbița waits outside the room.

Bebe does the job—inserting a probe into Găbița's uterus to stimulate a miscarriage—without anesthesia or guarantee that it will work, or even that Găbița will survive it.

With one ordeal half finished, another begins. Adi has pressured Otilia to come to his mother's birthday party. She leaves Găbița on the bed and gives her Adi's parents' phone number. At the parents' apartment, the phone rings but Otilia cannot get to it, and when she calls the hotel, Găbița doesn't pick up. Otilia extricates herself from the party and escapes into the dark city. Distant lights flicker; dogs bark. There is no cab; she takes the train. Arriving breathless at the hotel, she finds Găbița dozing. On the bathroom floor, in a blood-soaked towel, lies the fetus. Otilia stuffs the bundle into her handbag and runs back into the night. She finds an unlocked apartment building, dashes up the stairway, and drops it all down the trash chute.

Almost the entirety of *4 Months, 3 Weeks, and 2 Days* elapses in two locations: the shabby hotel room and the streets. The room is brightly and flatly lit; the shots are long and static. The outdoor scenes spin and carom; they're so dark as to be virtually illegible. Claustrophobia and terror, rigidity and chaos are the conditions of women's lives in a patriarchal police state.

Happening (2021), adapted by Audrey Diwan from Annie Ernaux's autobiographical novel *L'Événement*, also tells the story of an abortion under near total prohibition, this one in France in 1963. Annie (Anamaria Vartolomei) is a gifted and serious student, destined for university, the way out of a provincial life of perpetual labor and housework, like her parents'. When she gets pregnant, she knows what she must do. "I'd like a child someday," she tells a doctor, as if seeking pardon, "but not instead of a life."

Annie's torment, like Găbița's, is measured in passing time; the film is divided by gestational week. Two doctors refuse to help. "The law is unsparing. Anyone who helps can end up in jail. Including you," the first one tells her. The other prescribes a drug Annie thinks is an abortifacient but in fact strengthens the fetus.

Annie gets sicker, more fatigued, more panicked. She fails at school. She punches her belly, sticks a knitting needle into her cervix. At week nine, she travels to Marseille to see Maxime, the guy who got her pregnant. He is aloof. At the beach with Maxime's friends,

Annie swims far out—alone, in danger. Finally, he connects her with an acquaintance, who gives Annie the address of the woman who performed her own abortion, along with a password. Lifesaving intelligence passes from woman to woman like a water bucket at a fire, with as little excess interaction as possible.

The abortionist warns Annie that any noise will end the procedure. But it is so agonizing that a cry escapes her lips; the abortionist narrows her eyes but finishes. Unlike Bebe, who relishes his clients' abjection, this woman is just taking the necessary precautions of an illicit trade plied in a thin-walled apartment.

Annie's abortion takes two tries. After the second she expels the fetus into a toilet in the dorm; she implores a girl who finds her to cut the umbilicus hanging from her vagina. She blacks out and wakes up in the hospital, where the emergency is recorded as a (legal) miscarriage, not an abortion. Annie goes on to take the university exams, thanks to a stranger's trust, a dormmate's level-headedness—and luck.

In these two films, the abortion scenes are unflinching yet unsensational. The rooms are not sordid, the instruments are clean, the practitioners skilled. Găbița's and Annie's pain is unmistakable, as is the anxiety of possible exposure, not to mention injury or death. There is no need for melodrama.

As *4 Months* and *Happening* suggest, the more radically criminalized abortion is in a film's setting, the more detailed are the depictions of its logistics and mechanics. When abortion is legal, the stories, like their protagonists, have space to breathe. But legality is relative, and not every contemporary character has a lot of breathing room. The American features *Never Rarely Sometimes Always* (2020), *Grandma* (2015), and *Obvious Child* (2014) are all set in a period of de jure legalization and de facto restriction, between *Roe* and *Dobbs*. These films expose the unequal distribution of harm—and freedom—when bodily autonomy is accessible only to some people, in some places. And the less accessible abortion care is, the greater the burden on relationships.

Autumn (Sidney Flanigan), the protagonist of writer-director Eliza Hittman's understated yet wrenching *Never Rarely Sometimes Always*, is the wrong person in the wrong place: a pregnant working-class seventeen-year-old in rural Pennsylvania, a state with stringent restrictions, including parental consent. But because Pennsylvania abuts New York, she is not without options, and the journey to the city to get the abortion is the occasion for the casual bond with her cousin Skylar (Talia Ryder) to be forged solid through sacrifice and earned trust.

Having gotten pregnant by one of her classmates—the viewer does not know which boy is the father—Autumn finds her way to a crisis pregnancy center, a faux clinic where opponents of abortion try to persuade pregnant people to keep their babies. She is given a drugstore pregnancy test and a sonogram of her "baby," and is misinformed of its gestational age, wasting time she does not have. Autumn knows her parents will not give consent, so she and Skylar search the internet, make an appointment, and take a bus to New York. Expecting to return later that evening, Autumn learns at the clinic that she is too far along for a vacuum aspiration or medication abortion and must undergo a more complicated two-day procedure.

If she uses health insurance, the fee will show up on her parents' statement, so she hands over almost all the cash she's got.

The girls wander the city, schlepping their suitcases, eating little, sleeping on the subway. Out of curiosity or boredom, Skylar texts Jasper (Théodore Pellerin), a boy—older, cooler—who hit on them on the bus. They stay up most of the night, Jasper plying Sklyar with drinks, Skylar paying scant attention to either him or her cousin.

Skylar and Autumn speak rarely, and don't say much when they do. Their faces—Autumn's grave and Madonna-like, Skylar's conventionally pretty, never without lipstick and eyeliner—telegraph subtle but unarticulated emotional changes. They communicate through acts. In one scene they quarrel and Autumn storms off. In the next, Skylar is doing Autumn's makeup in a public bathroom. They are far from home in a huge, frenetic city. They are missing school and their supermarket cashier jobs; their parents are probably furious. But Skylar sticks by Autumn.

The trials a girl must undergo to realize a rational choice—"I'm not ready to be a mom," she tells Skylar—make the abortion a crucial narrative turning point. But the emotional climax of *Never Rarely* comes later. The girls return to Port Authority without money for the bus home. Skylar texts Jasper and goes off with him, leaving Autumn to wander the empty terminal and search the streets for her cousin. When she returns she glimpses Skylar behind a thick round pillar, making out with Jasper. From the other side of the pillar, Autumn taps Skylar's arm; Skylar reaches back and they clasp hands. As Jasper continues to kiss her, Skylar's face registers dissociation, then pained forbearance. Afterwards, Jasper withdraws cash from an ATM. Skylar promises to pay him back. He says he will text her. But both know the transaction is over.

WHERE THE POLITICS are blue, the darkness around abortion lifts. When it is a normal part of a young person's reproductive life, it is not a nonevent, but not a calamity either—a life enabler but not a life changer. Accordingly, the filmmakers who set their stories in legal-abortion states can push abortion from center stage and give friendship star billing.

In Paul Weitz's *Grandma* (2015), abortion is more MacGuffin than plot. An urgent need and a deadline—$630 for an abortion at 5:30 on the evening the action begins—send pregnant teenager Sage (Julia Garner) to her grandmother Elle (Lily Tomlin), a lesbian poet, for help. But Elle is broke, having cut up her credit cards to make a mobile. So the pair take off in Elle's beater on a quest. They are seeking cash, of course, but what they gain is mutual appreciation where there had been annoyance, and new protectiveness and loyalty between grandmother and granddaughter. There is even cautious reconciliation between Sage and her distracted and judgmental mother, Judy (Marcia Gay Harden) and between Judy and her mother, Elle. The abortion is so incidental that it takes place offscreen.

Obvious Child (2014) by writer-director Gillian Robespierre, is a genre of one, an abortion rom-com. More extraordinarily, the abortion and the romance have intertwined, happy endings. Donna Stern, a potty-mouthed New York standup comic (played by the

New York standup comic Jenny Slate) has a night-long drunken debauch with Max (Jake Lacy), which ends in unprotected sex and, Donna discovers later, pregnancy. "I remember seeing a condom," she sheepishly confesses to her best friend, Nellie (Gaby Hoffmann). "I just don't know, like, exactly what it did."

It is a stressful time in an already messy life. Donna's boyfriend has slept with her close friend and broken up with her. "I would love to just murder-suicide them," she grumbles into the mic, in a routine that goes from cringy to disastrous. The bookshop where she works closes. She is twenty-eight, still begging for laughs in a tiny dive bar, and drinking many nights away. Max is too preppy, too Vermont-y, too nice to be a plausible boyfriend. "He's so Christian. He's like a Christmas tree," she tells her friend Joey (Gabe Liedman), the programmer at the bar. "So be the angel on top!" he exhorts. "I'm not the angel on top. I'm the menorah on the top of the tree that burns it down," she replies.

The pregnancy contributes to what Donna calls an "emotional crisis." But the abortion is not a crisis. There is no anguished decision, no legal impediment. Her friends are unswervingly supportive, unambiguously feminist. "I never regret it," Nellie tells Donna about her own abortion, adding that Donna owes Max nothing, not even the information that his sperm has helped create a living embryo. "We already live in a patriarchal society where a group of weird old white men in robes get to legislate our cunts," Nellie declares, in what might be a tagline for every film about abortion. And when Donna finally unveils her plan to Max, he rises to the occasion—pays his half, accompanies her to the clinic, and even brings her flowers.

On the operating table, Donna looks content as the clinician works below. In the recovery room, she smiles at another patient, dressed like her in a pink hospital gown and booties, and the other woman smiles back. In the last scene, she and Max are hanging out on the couch while she recuperates, about to watch *Gone with the Wind*. It is as if ending the pregnancy has liberated her to fall in love.

For Donna, as for many young people—Annie, Sage, perhaps Găbiţa—abortion is a rite of passage. In choosing their own lives over those of their fetuses they are forced to assess their futures and assert that their goals are worth pursuing. Friends and family accompany them to the threshold of adulthood—whether a black-market abortionist's backroom or the door of a legal clinic—and bear witness as they pass through.

If women friends are heroes in these stories, the men are ciphers, cads, and villains. (Just doing what should be minimally expected of him makes Max a Supermensch.) As steadfast as the women are, the men are squirrelly. As resourceful as the women are, the men are clueless. Maxime washes his hands of Annie's mess. Găbiţa's lover—or whatever he was—is never mentioned.

Of course, unwanted pregnancy is the result of heterosexual sex. But sex—much less sexual love—rarely occurs in these films, and when it does it is almost always a contest of power.

For many of the men, the women's desperation is a sexual bonanza. When Annie approaches her friend Jean for help, he interrogates her pruriently and suggests they go to bed—why not, since she is already pregnant? Otilia gives Bebe her body as the premium for the extra months of Găbiţa's pregnancy. Skylar trades a make-out session for bus fare. Elle endures a kiss with a long-ago male lover in exchange for $500—before he learns its purpose and refuses to contribute.

Mistrust in their male intimates is the default emotion, and the men prove it is warranted. In *4 Months*, when an agitated Otilia tries to leave the party, Adi pulls her into his bedroom and demands she tell him what is going on, assuring her he will not get angry. But as soon as she informs him, he does. How can she take such a risk? Is she crazy?

As they spar, she begins to simmer. "And if I was pregnant, what would we do?"

"How can you talk about this now?" he pleads. "I don't see the point if you're not pregnant."

Suddenly, clarity: "I want to know what I can expect of you," she replies.

"You're saying I wouldn't help? . . . I said I'm against abortion because it's dangerous."

"What's your solution?" Otilia asks.

By the time she puts on her coat, the viewer knows Otilia is going to break up with Adi.

Misogyny is the smog through which these women navigate, a miasma of masculine moralism, disinterest, sexual opportunism—and violence. Bebe vibrates with it. When Elle insists Sage's ridiculous boyfriend contribute to the cost of the abortion, he threatens to "fuck [her] up" with his hockey stick. (Grandma whacks him in the balls with it and appropriates fifty bucks from his dresser drawer.)

And in three and a half quietly heartbreaking minutes, *Never Rarely* charts a continent of masculine power and misogyny extending from

Nellie's "old white men in robes" to the local enforcers in small-town high schools. On the second day at the clinic, the social worker administers a routine interview with Autumn. It is about "your relationships," she says. But the questions are not about relationships; they are about intimate partner violence. Each query names a harm and asks Autumn whether she has experienced it. The seriousness of harm escalates, from refusal to wear a condom to rape, and after each scenario come the four words that give the film its title: "Never? Rarely? Sometimes? Always?" Autumn pauses for a long moment each time, her eyes glancing sideways, upwards, downwards—everywhere but at the other person in the room.

The only aggression to which she can answer "never" is her partner messing with her birth control. To the rest she responds, "Sometimes?" The upspeak is not just a teenage girl's verbal tic. It signals emotional precarity, maybe shame.

"Your partner has threatened or frightened you. Never? Rarely? Sometimes? Always?"

No answer. Then: "Why are you asking me this?"

"I want to make sure that you're safe," says the social worker and asks again.

"Um, rarely?"

"Your partner has hit you, slapped you, or physically hurt you. Never? Rarely? Sometimes? Always?"

Autumn's lips tremble, her eyes grow blurry. She says nothing.

The social worker does not push; there are only a few more questions, she reassures. "Your partner has made you have sex when you didn't want to. Never? Rarely? Sometimes? Always?"

Autumn is now crying openly. She wipes her nose with the sleeve of her sweatshirt.

"I have just one more question for you, okay, Autumn?" A pause. "Has anyone forced you into a sexual act in your lifetime? Yes or no?"

"Uh . . . yeah." Barely audible, she has nonetheless spoken the words—a start.

Then Autumn goes in for the final phase of her abortion. The camera scans her body from half-exposed leg to pale, impassive face. A monitor beeps. The anesthesiologist preps her arm for the injection. The social worker holds her hand. The doctor asks her name, birth date, and what procedure she is having. Autumn answers the first two, then forgets—or blocks—the third question. The doctor repeats it. "I'm having an abortion," replies Autumn. It is a statement of informed consent. But it is also an affirmation, however tentative, of self. Hittman has described *Never Rarely* as "a narrative about a girl carrying around a lot of pain and burden, and the loneliness of it all." But Autumn is not alone. When she emerges into the waiting room, Skylar is there. "Are you okay?" she asks.

These films—*Never Rarely* and *4 Months* most of all—remind us of the lengths to which millions of pregnant people must go to realize the human right to bodily autonomy and the risks their friends take to help them. But sometimes the peril and trauma of the experience are too great for the friendship to survive. When Otilia returns to the hotel after disposing of the bloody bundle, the room is empty. Again, she searches frantically for Găbița, whom she finds in the dining room, looking at the menu. "I was hungry," explains Găbița, insensate to her friend's panic.

Otilia stares across the table. "You know what we're going to do?" she says. "We're never going to talk about this, okay?" Găbiţa nods. The waiter brings a plate full of meat and offal. Otilia drinks mineral water. She turns from Găbiţa, toward the camera. The film ends. Criminalization enforces silence, and institutionalized misogyny can splinter the bonds between women. The conclusion of *4 Months* is ambiguous, but it is not optimistic.

THE SHATTERING of social bonds is not just a side effect of anti-abortion law. Suspicion, paranoia, and isolation are among the intents. Vigilante enforcement may be written into the law, as it is in Texas, or it can be informal, generalized to everyone and anyone, as it was in France in 1963, Romania until 1989, in the United States before *Roe*—and now, after it. We know that many people continue to get abortions whether it is legal or not; they just get dangerous, illegal abortions. (Nationally, legal abortions have dropped to nearly zero in total-ban states but increased where they are legal—an overall decrease of 6 percent in the first six months after *Dobbs*. Long-term global trends show the opposite effect, however: In countries with fewer restrictions, abortions have declined since 1990—probably because of more liberal contraception laws and better sex education—and risen in more restrictive countries.) This is why it is critical to build networks of pro-abortion activists, lawyers, journalists, and providers, both lay and accredited, to maintain access to safe, mostly self-managed, abortion and reinforce the solidarity these laws seek to erode.

Two recent documentaries, *The Janes* (2022) and *Plan C* (2023), are portraits of what Rayah Feldman called, in 2011, feminist "humanitarian subversiveness"—humanitarian in that it offers aid and solace to individuals and subversive in that it transmits the message that the state cannot stop pregnant people and their helpers from doing what needs to be done. *The Janes*, by Tia Lessin and Emma Pildes, documents the eponymous Chicago collective that arranged or performed approximately eleven thousand clandestine abortions before *Roe*. *Plan C*, by Tracy Droz Tragos, follows a network of advocates, health care workers, medical and legal hotline operators, and providers of web-based information and referrals for self-managed abortions as they move into quasi-legal territory as distributors of abortion pills to people in red states. The film begins in Texas after SB 8 and ends as the leaked opinion in *Dobbs* foretells cataclysm. Bookending what can now be called the *Roe* Era, the two documentaries belie the fantasy that progress marches forever forward.

These films say a lot about the courage of individuals. But more than that, they are testaments to solidarity. Solidarity is a kind of sympathy; mutual aid can engender love in both the giver and receiver. But solidarity is not the same as friendship. It is mobilized by principle, not warm feelings—and that is its strength.

In any form of civil disobedience, individuals make personal decisions about how much risk they will tolerate (when they were caught in 1972, seven Janes each faced up to 110 years in prison; luckily, *Roe* nullified the indictments). But underground operations develop security measures to protect anonymity, providing a measure of safety that even clusters of friends like those who helped Brittni Silva cannot.

Agreed-on rules prevent people from carelessness and "just-once" exceptions. Group discipline is reinforced by the understanding that any one person's false move endangers everyone. When fear of surveillance and extreme punishment undermine the human instinct to help the people we love, solidarity can carry on.

The women who formed Jane came from the left, the antiwar and civil rights movements, and other movements for social, economic, and racial justice, including feminism. They were used to thinking and acting politically. Meanwhile, pregnant people were taking potentially fatal measures to end their pregnancies; septic abortion wards were full. "Sometimes there are unjust laws that need to be challenged," says one collective member in *The Janes*. Says another: "I couldn't see myself sitting on the sidelines." The collective made its members brave. "We were ordinary women, trying to save women's lives," recalls a third Jane, cheerfully. "But we were felons."

Plan C was filmed as abortion bans started pressing in on doctors and clinics prescribing and providing self-managed abortions, on the distributors the *Plan C* website links to, and on other volunteers and professionals who in some way abet medication abortions. The film shows the enormous dedication, skillful and generous collaboration, and mutual respect of the people working in these networks. But a strategic tension also builds, one that characterizes the whole reproductive justice movement post-*Dobbs*. Some want to take maximal advantage of irresolution in the law. "What's legal and what's not. . . . has to just be proven by doing it and finding that in fact nobody [comes] after you because [the law] probably won't stand," says Francine Coeytaux, cofounder, along with Elisa Wells and Amy Merrill, of Plan C. The legal ambiguity that Coeytaux wants to exploit is also what is staying the hands of hospital staff, leading to dangerously substandard ob-gyn care. "I get frustrated with everybody trying to follow the rules instead of what really needs to be done," says another speaker in the film. An underground distributor is packaging and sending out pills on her own, to avoid implicating anyone else. "I come from a long line of firefighters," she says. "The recognition of an emergency and the need to respond to it is something that is part of who I am."

Others in the film, like Robin Marty, operations director of the West Alabama Women's Center in Tuscaloosa, are as enraged and heartbroken about the bans as anyone. But, with abortion a criminal offense carrying penalties of up to ninety-nine years in Alabama, the clinic has no choice but to follow the law to the letter. Before the ban 95 percent of its patients were terminating pregnancies, with both surgical and medication abortions. Now the clinic provides full-spectrum reproductive health care, minus abortion, to low-income patients, who are already severely underserved in the state. But without the income from abortion, the thirty-year-old facility may have to close.

Some are just cautious. Planned Parenthood has been criticized for its exceedingly risk-averse corporate policies, leaving independent providers to shoulder the bulk of the clientele and the legal exposure. Other would-be organizers have interpreted "aiding and abetting" broadly, to include sharing any information publicly or privately about abortion. Communicating such caution can come across as fanning panic. In *Plan C*, Farah Diaz-Tello, senior counsel of the nonprofit If/When/How: Lawyering for Reproductive

Justice, warns that telling a friend about your abortion opens the door for that friend to tell someone else, who then informs the police. "If you tell somebody, you effectively told law enforcement," she says. Is she suggesting that people who have abortions confide in no one? That organizers shut up? "Organizing and mobilizing is really hard when you're scared and you're censored," says Coeytaux. Maybe the lawyers need reminding that the First Amendment hasn't been overturned—yet.

Survival before legalization depended on sharing secrets. Otilia tells Găbița that "we're never going to talk about this" again. But Găbița found Bebe by talking to other students, and it is not unlikely that she and Otilia will pass along censored intelligence, including warnings to avoid him. Speak-outs sparked the U.S. abortion rights movement.

Today, "Shout Your Abortion" and "I Will Aid and Abet Abortion" are becoming more than slogans on T-shirts. The abortion underground is acquiring the skills to keep ahead of a sophisticated surveillance state backed up by private snitches and litigants. But all the encryption in the world does not eliminate risk. Resistance movements are built on trust, and the power of the surveillance state rests in corroding the sense that strangers can count on each other. In these circumstances, the public sphere shrinks, and as the Silva case shows, even the family can be an abortion seeker's worst enemy.

It is important to remember that the Janes were not friends of the abortion patients they served. They asked for only the most essential identifying information and destroyed it afterward. *Plan C* shows a volunteer crying as she listens to a pregnant person telling her story on the phone—a person she will never meet. But if these helpers and their beneficiaries are not exactly friends, they are not exactly strangers either. They are sisters—or what we now call, more gender-inclusively, siblings. Siblinghood is where solidarity and friendship merge. We need it more today than we have in decades. The state can try to control our reproductive organs, but it cannot subjugate our hearts.

HOW MUCH DISCOMFORT IS THE WHOLE WORLD WORTH?

Kelly Hayes & Mariame Kaba

ORGANIZING IS NOT a process of ideological matchmaking. Most people's politics will not mirror our own, and even people who identify with us strongly on some points will often differ sharply on others. When organizers do not fully understand each other's beliefs or identities, people will often stumble and offend one another, even if they earnestly wish to build from a place of solidarity. Efforts to build diverse, intergenerational movements will always generate conflict and discomfort. But the desire to shrink groups down to spaces of easy agreement is not conducive to movement building.

The forces that oppress us may compete and make war with one another, but when it comes to maintaining the order of capitalism and the hierarchy of white supremacy, they collaborate and work together based on their death-making and eliminationist shared interests. Oppressed people, on the other hand, often demand ideological alignment or even affinity when seeking to interrupt or upend structural violence. This tendency lends an advantage to the powerful that is not easily overcome.

Put simply, we need more people. What do we mean by this? We are not talking about launching search parties to find an undiscovered army of people with already-perfected politics with whom we will easily and naturally align. Instead, organizing on the scale that our struggles demand means finding common ground with a broad spectrum of people, many of whom we would never otherwise interact with, and building a shared practice of politics in the pursuit of more just outcomes. It's a process that can bring us into the company of people who share our beliefs quite explicitly, but to create movements, rather than clubhouses, we need to engage with people with whom we do not fully identify and may even dislike. We can build upon our expectations of such people and negotiate protocols around matters of respect, but the truth is, we will sometimes be uncomfortable or even offended. We will, at times, have to constructively critique people's behavior or simply allow them room to grow. There will be other times, of course, when we have to draw hard lines, but if we cannot organize beyond the bounds of our comfort zones, we will never build movements large enough to combat the forces that would destroy us.

SOME GROUPS HAVE learned to navigate difference and animus out of necessity. Incarcerated people organizing within prisons, for example, often learn to put feuds, rivalries, and personal differences aside because they recognize the necessity of building with who is there.

As Kelly and organizer Ejeris Dixon wrote in *Truthout* in June 2020, when discussing solidarity in the face of right-wing violence and the rise of fascism:

> Not everyone we work with on a particular issue has to have deep ideological alignment with us. A skilled organizer should be able to work with people who aren't of their own choosing, including people they don't like. It's really as simple as being attacked by fascist police in the streets. Once the attack begins, there are two sides: armed police inflicting violence and everyone else. We need to be able to see each other in those terms, reeling in the face of unthinkable violence, scrambling to stay alive and uncaged, and doing the work to protect one another.

This will not come easily, because white supremacy and classism have forced many wedges between our communities. Great harms have been committed and very difficult conversations are needed, but refusing to do that work, in this historical moment, is an abdication of responsibility. It is no exaggeration to say that the whole world is at stake, and we cannot afford to minimize what that demands of us.

This is not to say that we should seek no respite from the messiness and occasional discomfort of large-scale movement work. We all need spaces where we can operate within our comfort zone. Whether these take the shape of a collective, an affinity group, a processing space, a caucus, or a group of friends, we need people with whom we can feel fully seen and heard and with whose values we feel deeply aligned. In such a violent and oppressive world, we are all entitled to some amount of sanctuary. Many organizers have tight-knit political homes, sometimes grounded in shared identity, in addition to participating in broader organizing efforts.

But broader movements are struggles, not sanctuaries. They are full of contradiction and challenges we may feel unprepared for.

Effective organizers operate beyond the bounds of their comfort zones, moving into what we might call their "stretch zone," when necessary. No one has to be able to work with everyone, but how far beyond the bounds of easy agreement can you reach? How much empathy can you extend to people who do not fully understand your identity or experience or who have not had the same access to liberatory ideas? How much discomfort can you navigate for what you believe is truly at stake?

These are not questions anyone can answer for you, as we must all make autonomous choices about who we connect and build with, but if we do not challenge ourselves to navigate some amount of discomfort, our political reach will have terminal limits. To expand the practice of our politics in the world, we have to be able to organize outside of our comfort zones. People whose words and ideas don't yet align with our own often need room to grow, and some people grow by building relationships and doing work—often in fumbling and imperfect ways.

Political transformation is not as simple as handing newcomers a new set of politics and telling them, "Yours are bad, use these instead." Instead, we will sometimes have to accompany people along messy transformational journeys. And we must also remember that no matter how far we have come, we are still on our own messy journeys, and our own transformations will continue as we grow.

TO DO THIS kind of work, a person has to hone multiple skills, including the ability to listen.

When people delve into activism, they often grapple with questions like, "Am I willing to get arrested?" when often the more pressing question for a new activist is, "Am I willing to listen, even when it's hard?"

For organizer and scholar Ruth Wilson Gilmore, it was her time in Alcoholics Anonymous that helped her transform her practice of listening. "The main thing that I learned," Gilmore told us, "especially in the first couple years that I was going to meetings, was the beauty of the rule against crosstalk. It was the best thing that ever happened to me, that I couldn't say shit to anybody. I had to listen, and I had to learn to listen." The urge to interject or object ran deep for Gilmore. "I've always been a nerd, yet I've always been a know-it-all," she told us, "so there's this tension between my nerdiness that wants to know everything and my know-it-all-ness that wants everybody to know that I know it all already."

At first, listening did not come easily—or feel particularly productive— to Gilmore. "I would sit in these meetings, and I listened to people talk, and listened to them, and listened to them, and at first I was like, 'I don't get this, I don't get this.' And so for me in the early days, it was just a performance of words. I mean, my main thing was, 'I won't drink when I leave this meeting. I won't drink, and I won't use.'"

But over time, Gilmore began to appreciate the role of listening in the group's collective struggle to avoid drugs and alcohol—even when she did not appreciate what was being said. "I would be getting more and more wound up, because there'd be the sexist guy going on about women and his wife, and then there'd be somebody else talking nonsense about whatever, [but I was] learning to just sit there, and listen, and keep my eye on the prize, which was not just that I wasn't going to drink but that the only way I could not drink was if all of us didn't drink."

Being committed to the sobriety of every person in the room, which meant listening to their story and being invested in their well-being, helped Gilmore develop a deeper practice of patience. "That was kind of this transformation for me that carried into the organizing that I already used to do before I got sober," she told us.

It is our ability to constructively engage with other people that will ultimately power our efforts. We have to nurture that ability and respect its importance in all of the ways that our society does not. And that skill of constructive engagement starts with listening.

Like so many other aspects of organizing, listening is a practice, and at times, it's a strategic one.

We might need to hear something true that makes us uncomfortable. Listening deeply makes space for that to happen. But even if the person who's talking is off base, we can often still learn by listening to them. Why do they feel the way they do? What sources informed or convinced them? What influences them? What strengthens their resolve? What makes them hesitant to get more involved or to engage more boldly? If you are in an organizing space together, how has that issue brought them into a shared space with you despite your differences? What points of agreement might you build upon? What is surprising about them? A good organizer wants to understand these things about the people around them, and you cannot truly understand these things about a person without listening.

Organizers will often repeat the maxim, "We have to meet people where they are at." It is difficult to meet someone where they're at when you do not know where they are. Until you have heard someone out, you do not know where they are, so how could you hope to meet them there? Relationships are not built through presumption or through the deployment of tropes or stereotypes. We must understand people as having their own unique experiences, traumas, struggles, ideas, and motivations that will inform how they show up to organizing spaces.

Some task-focused activists brush off activities that involve "talking about our feelings." This is a common sentiment among bad listeners. The fundamental skill of patiently absorbing another person's words in a respectful and thoughtful manner is desperately lacking in our society. For this reason, it is folly to expect this skill to manifest itself fully formed when it is most needed, such as in a heated meeting, if we are not building a greater culture of listening in our work.

A group culture that helps participants build their listening skills is an important component of successful organizing. Political education can create opportunities for people to practice listening to one another, without interruption, and interacting meaningfully with what others have contributed. For example, during the Great Depression, communist union organizers in Bessemer, Alabama, developed a practice of devoting thirty minutes of each meeting to political education. For thirty minutes, material would be read aloud—creating space to collectively listen while also allowing members who could not read the opportunity to hear the information. Members would then spend fifteen minutes discussing the material, listening to each other's thoughts in response to the work.

In organizing, we sometimes expect people, including ourselves, to shed the habits this society has embedded in us through sheer force of will, when in reality we all need practice. Activities that help us hone our practice of listening can make us better organizers, improve our personal relationships, and help us build stronger and longer-lasting movements.

AS WE WORK to build more sustainable movements, we must think hard about our strategies for responding when organizers make mistakes. Social media can often foster a "zero-tolerance" attitude about political ignorance or missteps. Platforms like Twitter have helped facilitate tremendous accomplishments in movement work, but they have also created an arena for political performance and critique that is often divorced from relationship building or strategic aims. For many people, social media is not an organizing tool but a realm of political performance and spectatorship. A trend has emerged in which some organizers will demand performances of solidarity and awareness on social media but then critique or even tear apart those performances when they fall short or are deemed insincere. As with reality television, favorites emerge, and people are sometimes voted off the island.

When the performance of solidarity via the replication of the right words or slogans becomes our central focus, it's not surprising that responses might read as empty or even insincere. Sloganizing is not organizing, and paying righteous lip service to a cause, in the preferred language of the moment, does not empty any cages or transform anyone's material conditions. Rather than fixating on the grammar of people's politics, we organizers must ask ourselves what we want people to do.

When debates arise around language, we must also understand the extent to which the language of dissent and liberation has shifted over time. The terms and jargon we use today do not represent an "arrival" at the "correct" words that were always out there, waiting to be found, while our predecessors flailed about in search of them. The language we uplift in movements today represents an unending process of grappling—a search for words that embody the experiences of oppressed people in relation to their history, their current conditions, and the culture they are presently experiencing. Policing language, as though our phrasing is written in law, misunderstands that pursuit and the purpose it serves. If these words merely exist to divide us into categories—those who can properly discuss ideas and those who cannot—what is their value in the pursuit of liberation?

While it is important to trouble terminology and to engage with its evolution, the mastery of language does not spur systemic change or alter anyone's material conditions. The concept of "allyship," for example, is often grounded in presentation rather than substantive action. Similarly, people who believe they are "good people" often view goodness as a fixed identity, evidenced by their expressed feelings about injustice rather than a set of practices or actions. Goodness, to them, is a designation to be defended rather than something that they seek to generate in the world in concert with other people. Mainstream liberals often fall prey to this line of thinking because liberal politics play very heavily into political identity as being determinant of whether a person is good or bad (Democrats are good, Republicans bad). But the left can fall into its own version of this trap by treating politics as a test of how well we can perform language or recite ideas.

Our movements are not driven by getting the words just right. They are driven by the goal of enacting change through collective struggle as we endeavor to both understand ideas and turn them into action. Fumbling is inevitable, but as Gilmore tells us, "practice makes different."

Dixon emphasizes that people will show up imperfectly and that organizers have to anticipate that mistakes and harm will happen. "I worry we're creating a culture now where people are so afraid to make mistakes," she told us. "They're afraid to not have the analysis before they open their mouth. The bonds that I'm really trying to build within organizing are the bonds where we can divulge the things that we are nervous about, or ashamed of, or the things we need to learn, all of those areas, because that's when I know we're building the kind of intimacy that takes care of each other around heightened threats."

Dixon points out that when trust is lost, organizing not only becomes more difficult, but it also becomes more vulnerable to surveillance and infiltration: "A huge piece of COINTELPRO was around seeding distrust." Therefore, she says, a key part of organizing is building bonds of trust, and that can only happen within a context where people are allowed to be vulnerable and make mistakes.

Learning and growing in front of other people can be embarrassing, and even intimidating, particularly for people who have been put down or made to feel diminished in the past. Even seasoned organizers like Dixon often worry about derailing their work with a verbal misstep. "I have a small crew of other organizers where I think our text thread is mostly questions we are afraid to ask publicly," she acknowledged. "It's our own little political education circle, where we ask, 'What does this mean?' Or, 'Is this fucked up?' Or, 'What is the right way to say this? Because I don't think this is right.'" Dixon says that she believes "everyone needs that text thread," but she also hopes that more of our movement spaces can operate in the same spirit and offer opportunities for people to "feel safe in their process of transforming."

Creating trust-based movement spaces also puts us in a better place to confront harm and conflict, Dixon says.

"The biggest part of the work is how we maintain relationships while navigating harm," she told us. "Because that's the thing, that will break your group. That'll break any project." Dixon stresses the importance of conflict resolution and accountability mechanisms within groups—that is, group- or community-based methods of confronting harm, such as peace circles and transformative justice. But she also reminds us that in order for accountability mechanisms to serve their purpose, people need room and opportunities to grow. "People need to build skills and mechanisms to navigate conflict. Sometimes we're not apologizing. Sometimes we're not accountable.

Sometimes we have done harmful things. Sometimes we're doing things we were never told go against the norms [of the group] and then are being held accountable."

In an organizing space, accountability should not be about policing or punishment, but our punitive impulses can sometimes twist accountability mechanisms into those shapes. It's easy to forget how imperfectly we ourselves have shown up in movement spaces and throughout our lives. Sometimes our aggravation with others is rooted in pain or trauma we have experienced; sometimes it is rooted in our uneasiness about things we may have said or done that were equally upsetting because we did not always know what we know now. And regardless of how much we believe we have learned, as the saying goes, we don't know what we don't know. Many of us would not be in this work today if someone along the way had not been patient with us.

Even if we never develop a sense of mutual respect and under-standing, or even come to like the people we're working with, we can still build power with them. In many cases, we must. After all, the whole world is at stake. We must ask ourselves, how much discomfort is the whole world worth?

CONTRIBUTORS

Gaiutra Bahadur is Associate Professor of Journalism and English at Rutgers University–Newark and author of *Coolie Woman: The Odyssey of Indenture.*

Rev. Dr. William J. Barber II is Founding Director of the Center for Public Theology and Public Policy at Yale Divinity School and Co-Chair of the Poor People's Campaign. His latest book is *We Are Called to Be a Movement.*

Dan Berger is Associate Professor of Comparative Ethnic Studies at the University of Washington Bothell. His latest book is *Stayed on Freedom: The Long History of Black Power through One Family's Journey.*

Charisse Burden-Stelley is Associate Professor of African American Studies at Wayne State University. Her latest book is *Black Scare/Red Scare: Theorizing Capitalist Racism in the United States.*

Jodi Dean is Professor of Politics at Hobart and William Smith Colleges. Her most recent book is *Comrade: An Essay on Political Belonging.*

Nathan R. DuFord is Assistant Professor of Government at Smith College and author of *Solidarity in Conflict: A Democratic Theory.*

nia t. evans is a freelance writer and fellow at *Mother Jones.* Her writing has also appeared in *Hammer and Hope* and *Dissent.*

Alex Gourevitch is Associate Professor of Political Science at Brown and author of *From Slavery to the Cooperative Commonwealth.*

Kelly Hayes is a Menominee organizer and writer. She is coauthor, with Mariame Kaba, of *Let This Radicalize You: Organizing and the Revolution of Reciprocal Care.*

Juliet Hooker is Professor of Political Science at Brown. Her latest book is *Black Grief/White Grievance: The Politics of Loss.*

Daniel Martinez HoSang is an organizer and Professor of American Studies at Yale. His most recent book is *A Wider Type of Freedom: How Racial Justice Liberates Everyone.*

Leah Hunt-Hendrix is cofounder of the Solidaire Network and Way to Win. She is coauthor, with Astra Taylor, of the forthcoming book *Solidarity: The Past, Present, and Future of a World-Changing Idea.*

Mie Inouye is Assistant Professor of Political Studies at Bard College and Curriculum Co-Director of the National Political Education Committee of the Democratic Socialists of America. A political theorist and organizer, she has also written for *Jacobin* and *The Forge.*

Mariame Kaba is an organizer and founder of Project NIA, which works to end youth incarceration. Her latest book, coauthored with Kelly Hayes, is *Let This Radicalize You: Organizing and the Revolution of Reciprocal Care.*

Judith Levine is a feminist journalist, essayist, and activist. Her most recent book, with Erica R. Meiners, is *The Feminist and the Sex Offender: Confronting Sexual Harm, Ending State Violence.*

David Roediger is the Foundation Professor of American studies at the University of Kansas. His most recent book is *The Sinking Middle Class.*

Sarah Schulman is a queer writer and activist. Her most recent book is *Let the Record Show: A Political History of ACT UP New York, 1987–1993.*

Michael Simmons, a human rights activist and former member of the Student Nonviolent Coordinating Committee, is codirector of the Ráday Salon.

Gwendolyn Zoharah Simmons is Professor Emerita in African American, Women's, and Religious Studies at the University of Florida and a former member of the Student Nonviolent Coordinating Committee.

Astra Taylor is a filmmaker, writer, and cofounder of the Debt Collective. She is coauthor, with Leah Hunt-Hendrix, of the forthcoming book *Solidarity: The Past, Present, and Future of a World-Changing Idea.*

Rev. Dr. Liz Theoharis, an ordained minister in the Presbyterian Church (USA), is Director of the Kairos Center at Union Theological Seminary and Co-Chair of the Poor People's Campaign. Her latest book is *Cry Justice.*

Simon Torracinta is Lecturer in History of Science at Harvard and a contributing editor at *Boston Review*. His writing has also appeared in *n+1* and *The New Inquiry.*

Ege Yumuşak, a charter member of Harvard's Graduate Student Union, is a postdoctoral fellow and lecturer in philosophy at Columbia. Her writing has also appeared in *The Forge, The Point,* and *The Drift.*